Understanding Accounting in a Changing Environment

Understanding Accounting in a Changing Environment

Anthony Hopwood
London School of Economics

Michael Page
University of Southampton

Stuart Turley
University of Manchester

Prentice Hall

In association with

The Institute of Chartered Accountants in England and Wales

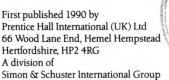

First published 1990 by
Prentice Hall International (UK) Ltd
66 Wood Lane End, Hemel Hempstead
Hertfordshire, HP2 4RG
A division of
Simon & Schuster International Group

This book consists of a research study undertaken on behalf of The Institute of Chartered Accountants in England and Wales. In publishing this book the Institute considers that it is a worthwhile contribution to discussion but neither the Institute nor the Research Board necessarily shares the views expressed, which are those of the authors alone.

No responsibility for loss occasioned to any person acting or refraining from action as a result of any material in this publication can be accepted by the authors or publisher.

Printed and bound in Great Britain by
BPCC Wheatons Ltd, Exeter.

Library of Congress Cataloging-in-Publication Data

Understanding accounting in a changing environment / edited by Anthony
   Hopwood. Michael Page. Stuart Turley.
     p. cm.
   "Prentice Hall in association with the Institute of Chartered
Accountants in England & Wales."
   Includes bibliographical references.
   ISBN 0−13−947524−9 : $40.00
   1. Accounting—Great Britain—Congresses. I. Hopwood, Anthony G.
II. Page, Michael. III. Turley, Stuart. IV. Institute of Chartered
Accountants in England and Wales.
HF5616.G7U54   1990
657'.0941—dc20   89-23173
                                            CIP

British Library Cataloguing in Publication Data

Understanding accounting in a changing environment.
   I. Hopwood, Anthony, *1944−* II. Page, Michael, *1950−* III.
Turley, Stuart
657
ISBN 0-13-947524-9

---

1 2 3 4 5   94 93 92 91 90

Contents

Foreword

The 'Understanding a Changing Environment' Project (UCE) was initiated by the Research Board of the Institute of Chartered Accountants in England and Wales towards the end of 1984. It was a project which differed in kind from those usually sponsored by the Research Board. Instead of being directed towards the illumination of a particular (accounting) problem or problem area, the UCE project aimed to throw light on the effect of uncertainty and change on the environment in which accounting will have to survive — and hopefully flourish — during the last decade of this century and the early part of the next. It was a formidable assignment.

The initiative for the project came from within the Institute and was a recognition of the need to get the longer term future on the agenda, unfettered by shorter term policy making considerations. In order to generate as broad as possible a spectrum of ideas, an Understanding a Changing Environment Group (UCEG) was established, involving some twenty-five individuals from a wide variety of backgrounds, both accounting and non—accounting. The Group met on nine occasions over a two-year period from Spring, 1985. Presentations were made by 'outsider' specialists as well as by members of the Group and were usually followed by spirited and lengthy discussions. Much of the credit for the undoubted success of the meetings must go to Professor Anthony Hopwood for his sterling efforts in attracting an excellent portfolio of speakers with the right mix of experience and vision in the areas being discussed.

The summarized results of the presentations and discussions at the meetings of the UCEG are contained in this book. They provide a rich and fascinating tapestry of the thinking of men and women at the forefront of their fields. Many organizations in both the private and public sectors are actively preparing for the future through planning groups' strategy reviews. Although these processes are continuous they can sometimes be dominated by immediate concerns such as getting next year's budgeted income statement and balance sheet right! The contents of this book provide a broader and longer term perspective which should encourage and assist the managers of organizations to devote at least some of their valuable 'planning' time to a consideration of the strategic implications over the next twenty years or so of an environment which is likely to change in ways and at a pace which are impossible to predict with any degree of precision but which it is likely to be fatel to ignore.

The Research Board and the Institute are indebted to Anthony Hopwood, Michael Page and Stuart Turley for their efforts in coordinating the work of the UCE, and to all those members of the Group and occasional presenters who ensured that the efforts of the organizers were so worthwhile.

John Arnold
Director of Research
Institute of Chartered Accountants in England and Wales.

Acknowledgements

This volume is the outcome of a project to which a large number of people have made significant contributions. The stimulus for many of the ideas which are reported here came from the discussions of the Understanding a Changing Environment Group and the provocative presentations by the speakers at the Group's meetings. We are particularly grateful to the individual members of the Group for maintaining interest and commitment to the project throughout its two-year period. The continuity this provided was a great asset in dealing with the issues addressed. We also wish to recognize the vision and commitment of the Institute of Chartered Accountants in England and Wales (ICAEW) office holders, in particular the Secretary, John Warne, the Research Board and the then Director of Research, Bryan Carsberg, in promoting and sponsoring the project. Members of the Institute's secretariat commented helpfully on reports and papers as the project progressed and we are grateful for their contribution. A large debt of gratitude is due to those who provided secretarial support for the project — Anne Gleeson for her great care in dealing with the arrangements for the group meetings and, together with Hilary Garraway, for undertaking the word processing in the production of this book.

Anthony Hopwood
Michael Page
Stuart Turley

PART ONE

Dealing with Change

1

Introduction and Summary

The accounting profession is in the midst of the greatest period of change we
have ever known. Changing times like these present seemingly insurmountable
obstacles. But changing times also present unlimited opportunities.
(R.E. Larson, President, Financial Accounting Foundation (USA),
January 1986)

Obstacles or opportunities — how should the accounting profession
classify and react to the very considerable challenges and changes
that it is currently facing? During the 1980s, issues of change have
dominated the agendas of professional bodies and members of the
profession, in public practice, in industry and finance and in the
public sector. Illustrations of significant aspects of change are easy
to find: the structure of the profession in the United Kingdom;
educational demands, and the increasing variety of skills required by
accountants; the technological environment in manufacturing,
financial services, and in information recording and transmission;
the shifting boundary between the private sector and government
activity; and the criteria and standards against which organizational
behaviour and performance are to be assessed.

Undeniably, the United Kingdom in the late 1980s is very
different from what it was in the 1970s. As uncertainty increases, as
the pace of change quickens, and as developments are exploited in
a manner which imposes high costs on those late to react, understanding the nature of change as it affects the accounting profession
has become ever more important. Whether change is a temporary or
a continuing phenomenon, the profession's response should be based
on a proper appreciation of the critical components of its environ-

ment and on those changes which are likely to have most impact overall on accountants.

The Understanding a Changing Environment Project

During the latter part of 1984, the Research Board of the Institute of Chartered Accountants in England and Wales (ICAEW) initiated a project entitled Understanding a Changing Environment. The Project, which began in January 1985, was based on the meetings of a discussion group, each concerned with particular aspects of change affecting the accounting profession. The Understanding a Changing Environment Group (UCEG) was intended to provide a broad forum in which the implications of economic, technical and social change for the future development of the profession could be explored.

The primary role of the Project was one of helping to illuminate the background to policy issues, by providing information and ideas about ways in which the accounting environment might change over the next twenty years, by exploring possible scenarios and their implications, and by seeking to identify the structural links and factors which would be the important determinants of the future of accounting and professionally qualified accountants. So the UCEG operated not as a decision making or policy making group, nor as a forecasting group attempting to predict the future, but as a study group trying to open the difficult issues and assist the profession to incorporate explicit thinking about uncertainty and the future into its debates and policies.

Structure

The UCEG comprised a membership of about twenty-five individuals drawn from a wide variety of backgrounds. Its members included the office-holders of The Institute of Chartered Accountants in England and Wales, members in professional practice, in industry, in the financial sector, and in the public sector, members of parliament, individuals from government departments, and academics. There were a few changes in the membership of the Group during the project, with new members being added where necessary, but a large core remained throughout the two-year period of meetings. The full list of all those who were members is included in Appendix 1.

The meetings of the UCEG spanned the period Spring 1985 to Spring 1987. A total of nine meetings was held, covering both general developments in the environment and more specific issues for the profession. The general structure of the meetings involved presentation by one or more speakers (members of the group and others) followed by an open discussion by the Group. The nature of the Project, involving a wide choice of topics and relatively unstructured debates (meetings could be five hours long), meant that there was an opportunity to discuss the broad significance of issues, as well as more detailed implications.

Topics

While the agenda of topics discussed in the Project meetings was not fixed in advance, the basic nature of what would be relevant was recognized. It was clear at the outset that it would be important for the Group to look at general changes in the business environment, as well as specific matters of technical importance to the accounting profession. Overall the meetings followed a pattern of moving from more general topics to specific issues in the accounting and financial environment.

The first two sessions were devoted to consideration of the broad economic and social development of the United Kingdom, topics which at first thought might seem far removed from the basic concerns of accountants, but which are important when looking at the structural linkages on which the future is dependent. More specific topics were then selected. First, the major organizational or functional divisions within accountancy were covered by sessions looking at the development of professional firms and the future of accountants in the finance function in industry. Information technology was regarded as an important topic as it affects so much organizational activity linked to accounting, as well as wider aspects of production technology and the financial markets. The regulatory role of the profession was examined in a meeting devoted to accounting standard setting, and finally the broader issues of regulation of financial activity were covered in a discussion on City regulation.

Concerned as it was with the future, the Group also gave early consideration to the question of *how* we think about the future. One session of the UCEG looked at the ideas of scenario planning as a means of approaching an uncertain future. At a later stage a number of specific accounting scenarios were debated and their implications assessed.

The subjects covered in the UCEG series of meetings are set out in Table 1.1, and the speakers are listed in Appendix 2.

Table 1.1 Topics for the UCEG meetings

General topics	The economic future
	Social futures
Ways of looking at the future	Scenario planning
Specific issues	Professional firms
	The accountant in industry
	Information technology
	Accounting standard setting
	City regulation
Overview	Scenarios for the accounting profession

Reporting on the Project

The structure and content of this book reflects the agenda of the subjects considered within the Understanding a Changing Environment Project.

In Chapter 2 a number of accountancy scenarios for the future are presented, which attempt to synthesize different subjects and experiment with the approach of scenario planning. Chapters 3—9 then report on individual topics, based on the presentations and discussions from the UCEG series of meetings. The final chapter gives an overview of the exercise and the insights it has provided.

In line with the way in which the role of the UCEG was originally envisaged, the objective of this book is to promote future thinking by raising issues, not to provide speculative forecasts and predictions. We hope that this volume will encourage recognition of the uncertainty in the accountancy environment, and of the need to question assumptions about the relationships between accountancy and its environment, as it is these assumptions which will determine the approach of the profession to future issues.

Summary of Principal Issues

In this section the principal issues arising from the discussion of the topics described earlier are summarized. However, rather than list a series of issues under each topic heading, the summary points set out below attempt to reflect the links between different topics, the issues which recurred in the discussions on separate subjects, and the significant factors which are evident from consideration of the past development of accounting. Each point is stated with just a few brief comments for the purposes of explanation.

1. *An expanding demand for services*
The need for new types of information, reflecting changing societal preferences, means the profession will be expected to, or at least will be given the opportunity to, develop additional roles. The profession is faced with challenges to develop accounting measurement to cover an expanding domain. There is a need for new forms of economic calculation and independent assessment which operationalize broader concepts of value and performance, such as organizational efficiency, reflect changing financial relationships and activity, and meet apparent deficiencies in existing measurement systems.

   This trend is likely to be most evident in public interest organizations and public sector activities. In one direction, it could be exemplified by the possibility that, through reporting changes, regulation, or the recognition by the courts of liability, accounting firms could be forced to act more as guarantors of the financial condition of companies. Additionally, wider responsibilities to search for fraud and irregularities and to report to regulatory agencies may fundamentally alter the relationships between auditors and their clients.

2. *Developing new services within firms*
In addition to (1) above, professional firms are themselves seeking to promote demand by developing new services and entering new markets. For example, there has been considerable discussion recently regarding attempts to 'redefine' the content of the audit service, and firms have diversified into many new activities in recent years. Such changes challenge and stretch the definition and boundary of what is to be regarded as 'accounting', that is, the activity of the accounting profession.

3. Internationalization

One of the most significant changes in the accounting environment is that it is increasingly international. An increasing number of professional accounting firms are themselves multinational partnerships or affiliations and they and their clients are subject to regulations set at a transnational level. Accountants will be forced to consider the effects of a more international economy, both within Europe and more globally, and expectations of the accounting profession for the 'exporting' of services.

4. The competitive environment

The development of public practice in a competitive environment raises issues to do with competition between firms within the profession. While the effects of changes in competitive practices in recent years may take some time to assess, it is likely that the nature of competition will become increasingly unstable in the future.

In addition, issues arise regarding the position of accountants in relation to other professional groupings, with implications for the staffing structures and expertise of firms.

5. The growth of firms and the role of the Institute

In an environment characterized by the above points, it is unlikely that the growth of firms will be constrained by a lack of available work. However, there will be significant shifts in the mix of work by different firms and different sizes of firms. This change could place pressure on the relationship between the Institute and the firms and their activities, as the commonality of services offered declines and the 'culture' of firms becomes more variable. Such pressure will also grow as the membership of firms becomes less linked to professional qualification. Given this diversity of activity, a recognition of specializations may become more critical.

6. Competition and public interest

The success of the profession relies on public perceptions of its members' abilities and roles. Traditionally the profession has claimed allegiance to the concept of serving the public interest. Developing the content of services has to be set alongside other values regarding quality of service, e.g. independence. There may be increasing use of the courts to define the elusive concept of the 'public interest' and the potential liability of accountants more explicitly.

7. Accountants in industry

The changing nature of the industrial finance function confronts the accounting profession with two challenges for the future:

(a) Skills. The changing role of traditional management accounting skills, the shifting role of economic calculation within organizations, the impact of information technology, and changes in management decision making and risk taking may all require a different set of skills and aptitudes from those traditionally supplied by the profession. Education, training and qualification requirements hold an important key to the markets and opportunities that will be open to professionally trained accountants and firms.

(b) Recruitment. Historically, public practice has provided a major source of supply of qualified recruits to industrial management. In the short term the majority of organizations will still have to look to the profession for the supply of staff, but in the longer term there is the possibility of challenge from the development of a separate managerial profession. Education, training and qualification requirements hold an important key to the markets and opportunities that will be open to professionally trained accountants and firms.

8. *Technology*

The effects of changing technology are all-pervasive. It has an impact on professional firms, in their staff skills and staffing structures, and the technology of their work, as well as that of their clients. It has an impact on industry and commerce, changing the nature of design and manufacturing, and in some contexts, such as financial markets, changing the very nature of transactions. The power of information processing and storage in databases may ultimately change the basis of financial reporting.

9. *The regulatory environment*

The accounting profession has enjoyed the benefits of a position in which the state has relied upon the profession for certain functions arising out of state regulation of commercial activity. As the involvement of the state changes, the balance in this relationship also shifts. Both the extent of regulation and the degree to which it emphasizes detailed rules and definitions rather than general concepts are important. The profession will need to adapt to the changing structure and content of regulation.

10. *Regulation by the accounting profession*

Within the general regulatory framework, the profession has responsibilities for regulation of its members' own activities and for the development of regulations or norms in the form of accounting standards, which are intended to influence the behaviour of others outside the profession. The visibility of both these functions is likely to increase. In the former area it may be difficult to avoid outside involvement in self-regulatory processes, particularly as international comparisons and pressures are applied. In the latter case perceptions in the financial community of the benefits of accounting standards will be critical and the problems of legitimacy and enforcement must be addressed. Auditing regulations are likely to become of increasing importance.

11. *Education*

Many of the above points have significant implications for the education and training of accountants. They affect the portfolio of skills required to meet the demands of the changing environment and the structure of the educational process by which these skills are acquired. A failure by the profession to train its members in broad management skills could lead to loss of the profession's current high status and a retreat into narrow functional specialization. Particular questions include the need to adhere to a common skill base for all accountants and the possibility of specialist qualifications either as part of, or in addition to, the basic accountancy qualification. The education offered to new recruits will be an important determinant of the profession's future. Providing the appropriate education and training will be crucial as the profession seeks to attract students from a declining number of 18—21 year olds.

Final Comments

The objective of the Understanding a Changing Environment Project was to examine the underlying relationships between accounting and its environment which will determine the future, and to identify the issues flowing from those relationships which the profession should consider if it is to continue to be adaptable and to develop.

The eleven items above will clearly not provide a comprehensive list of all matters concerning the future for accountants, but it represents, on the basis of the extensive discussions of the UCEG, a possible agenda from which interested groups, individual firms and professional groupings in the accounting community can begin to consider current and future change. Many of the issues raised are already under consideration within the Institute, and the practical implications of a number of such issues have changed in nature since the UCEG discussed them. For example, the debate on the structure of the profession was advanced considerably with the moves by the English and Scottish Institutes towards unification, the influence of internationalization is now seen more clearly in the light of developments towards a single market in the European Community, and proposals for development of the system of education and training have been prepared.

However, even as individual instances of change are dealt with, the general issues must continue to be given prominence if the profession's response and development is to be appropriate to the underlying character of the accounting environment.

2

Future Scenarios for the Accounting Profession

When considering the various specific issues which will be significant in the future development of the accounting profession, it is also important to review how these issues can be taken into account in the process of planning itself.

For many people, planning and forecasting are the same thing, but in order to prepare successfully for anything other than the very short term future, it is vital to start with the recognition that a forecast, in the sense of a single best guess about individual facets of the future, is almost certain to be wrong. The Arab proverb 'Those who foretell the future lie, even if they are right' sums up this idea, because even though forecasts may often be right they will be wrong just when they are needed most; forecasts fail to anticipate discontinuities and major changes.

If the environment is very uncertain, extrapolation of past trends to make future predictions may be little better than pure speculation, and the emphasis of planning should be on ensuring the flexibility of the organization itself to cope with uncertainty.

Where arriving at a 'best guess' is unlikely to be helpful, what then is a sensible way of preparing for the future? This chapter approaches the uncertainty present in the environment by using scenario analysis to illustrate some of the major uncertainties facing the profession and to evaluate their implications. The scenarios build upon the examination of individual specific issues in other chapters by describing more general pictures in which the interactions between different issues can be examined.

Scenario Planning

The term 'scenario' has become part of modern-day jargon in a variety of contexts. Some definition is therefore required of how this term has been interpreted in the present exercise. Two definitions which illustrate the approach adopted are:

descriptions of possible future worlds; worlds in which the consequences of alternative strategic choices made today may be examined (Leemhuis, 1985); and

hypothetical sequences of events constructed for the purposes of focussing attention on causal processes and decision points (Sims and Eden, 1984).

These definitions emphasize that the objective of the exercise is not to develop pictures of the future simply as a means of improving the quality of the debate in professional circles, but, rather, to provide a vehicle for analysing important policy choices facing the profession in the present. Three scenarios are outlined in the chapter. They are intended to be illustrative and do not purport to predict the future. The scenarios are constructed to provide questions not answers.

Many companies and other organizations have paid lip-service to scenario planning, but a lot of them have had little success in their attempts, often because they have merely quantified possible ranges for different variables. In order to make scenario planning effective it is important to convert these 'first-generation' scenarios into 'decision' scenarios and to 'involve management, top and middle, in the unfolding business environment much more intimately than would be the case in the traditional planning process' (Wack, 1985). Scenarios must be based on sound analysis. They must probe into the factors underlying change rather than merely focus on their presumed immediate consequences. The aim must always be to change decision makers' perceptions about how the world works.

An important decision which must be taken at the outset is the time frame with reference to which the scenarios are to be developed. Three different general approaches to choosing the planning horizon can be identified, as shown in Table 2.1 (Leemhuis 1985). For the present exercise, a medium-term planning horizon was adopted, looking to the period up to the end of the century.

By 'archetypal scenarios' is meant descriptions of alternative developments in economic performance and structures and other

Table 2.1 Planning horizons for scenarios

Approach	Planning horizon	Scenarios
Short-term	5 years	Business cycle
Medium-term	10-15 years	Archetype
Very long-term	over 15 years	Exploratory

socio-political and technological factors. They represent 'broad brush' outlines of future environments.

The key to constructing valid scenarios is the identification, and analysis of the consequences, of predetermined elements — those events which have already happened, or which are almost certain to happen, which will create the future. Predetermineds can arise from many sources, for example they can be climatic, demographic, geophysical, social, political or economic. Heavy rain in the Himalayas means that there will be flooding in the lower Ganges some days later; a fall in the birthrate means that there will be fewer children entering schools five years later, and so on. Every business faces a wide range of predetermined elements, but identifying them and evaluating their significance may be difficult. Some of the great planning disasters of business history (e.g. the Ford Edsel) can be seen to have arisen from erroneous identification of predetermineds (Drucker, 1985, p.45).

Using the Scenarios in Planning

The technique of scenario planning is useful only if it results in some insights which are relevant to actual decisions being made. The present chapter does not make specific recommendations on planning policy, but places emphasis on providing descriptions of possible futures against which those with responsibility for strategic decisions can evaluate alternative policies, taking account of their own objectives and preferences. In this way the scenarios can have relevance to members of the Institute and others in a wide variety of backgrounds who are concerned to identify the challenges of the future in their own particular context.

The framework set out in Figure 2.1 describes what is required of decision makers to make use of scenarios in strategic planning. Section A relates to what is reported in this chapter, namely the development of a number of plausible scenarios and identification of the key variables driving the future. Sections B and C describe the steps required of decision makers. These involve identifying long-term objectives, alternative strategies and criteria for choice between them, and evaluating the strategies under the different scenarios. What is important is that the decision makers should utilize their own perceptions and expectations regarding how they think key variables might develop within the scenarios, as a basis for comparing the results of the alternative strategies with the desired objectives.

The Example of Oil

A good example of the successful application of scenario planning is to be found in the recent history of the oil industry, where, after many years of smooth compound growth up to 1973, most large oil companies assumed that they could project the pattern of their business indefinitely, but, as is well known, the oil price shocks of 1973 and 1979 invalidated prior projections of oil prices and the demand for oil. This example is based on accounts of these events reported in Wack (1985) and Lorenz (1980).

In the early 1970s Wack and other planners in the Royal Dutch Shell group of companies (Shell) were able to identify the energy gap which would develop between the demand for oil and the willingness of oil-producing countries to sell it at the prevailing price set by the Teheran agreement. Shell planners examined the outlook for oil-producing countries, oil-consuming countries and oil companies. The results of these examinations showed that individual oil-producing countries would behave in different ways — Iran, with reserves which would soon begin to decline rapidly, would seek to raise prices to conserve oil for its future needs, Saudi Arabia would find that it could not absorb the funds generated from oil sales and would see that its best investment would be oil in the ground.

On the other hand, oil-consuming countries were becoming more dependent than ever on imported oil — Japan had no reserves of indigenous energy and the United States had been providing the majority of its growth in energy requirements from imported oil for

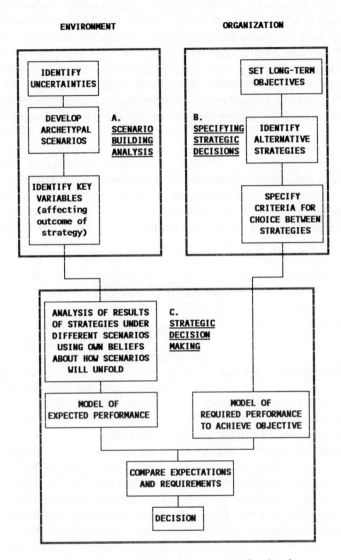

Figure 2.1   Using scenarios in strategic planning

some time and would need to do so increasingly as its own oil production had peaked and would soon begin to decline. The current level of economic activity was thus dependent on continued availability of abundant oil. Shell planners found that the 'surprise-free' scenario of continued orderly growth was incompatible with existing predetermined elements, and predicted that an oil-price shock would occur. The supply of oil would become negatively price-elastic; as prices rose, sellers would need to sell less.

In the oil industry in 1973, Shell planners found it was not easy to convince people engaged in exploration and production that much of their income would be lost as producing countries' governments took over control. Equally, in refining, transporting and marketing, where high growth had ensured that any over-investment was only temporary, the message that the industry was now to become a low growth one was not welcome. Nevertheless, Wack demonstrates that, in Shell at least, the message was accepted.

Building Blocks for Accounting Scenarios

In looking to the future, it is first of all important to have an understanding of the variables which have interacted in the past to shape accounting. In this section, a number of factors, which have been important determinants of the development of accounting and the accounting profession, are examined, to provide the basis for the creation of the scenarios. Each factor is considered in terms of both its historical role and possible future conditions that could be postulated.

The Economic Environment

The development of accounting could be expected to be linked to general economic growth. It is possible to associate the rise of accounting with economic developments in the nineteenth century. In recent years, however, professional accounting firms have enjoyed higher rates of growth than the economy in general, possibly reflecting the ability of accountants to exploit those specific areas of the economy which provide above-average opportunities at any point in time, rather than following general economic performance, although specific accounting issues may reflect particular economic factors.

The two extremes of reasonable feasibility were taken as:

1. Moderate international growth and moderate UK performance. Both the world economy and that of the United Kingdom might grow at, say, 3 per cent.

2. Poor international growth and poor UK performance. The world economy might grow at only 1—2 per cent and the UK economy would have almost nil growth.

The significant economic factors which could influence the future development of accounting are the continuing shift from manufacturing to services and the internationalization of the economy. The success of the services sector in general, and the City and financial services in particular, will be of crucial importance in overall economic performance, given the growth of international financial centres and the economic influence of the Pacific Basin. Low economic growth will mean that measurement of economic performance will remain important, but the growth in services may raise new measurement issues. While recognizing the importance of general economic performance, the lessons of the past are that the performance of the accounting profession has not been constrained by economic growth and that in looking to the future, national economic variables should not be regarded as the sole determinants of accounting development. Rather than general economic performance it is appropriate to consider the specific areas of activity which offer opportunities to the accounting profession.

Government and the State

The role given to accounting by the state has been a major influence on the development of accounting and the actions and needs of the state have provided the basis for many of the activities of the profession. This is likely to continue and should be taken account of in future planning.

State regulations, for example, in the areas of auditing, taxation, insolvency and, more recently, value for money in the public sector, have provided business opportunities for accountants. The services provided by accountants in public practice, and the developments of accounting activities within organizations, can often be traced to responses to initiatives by, or requirements of, the state. Further, in some areas, notably the statutory audit, the state has 'reserved' certain activities for the accounting profession in the sense that only members of specific accounting bodies can carry out those functions. The reserved functions provide commercial opportunities for accountants but also have an important role in defining the core activities which characterize accounting as a profession. The general structure of the regulatory environment imposed by the state has also placed power in the hands of the accounting profession, and has given emphasis to the exercise of professional judgement in the interpretation of statute.

Alternatives can be envisaged in terms of both the general approach to regulation and specific requirements. The general approach of the regulatory regime is important as this will affect government's attitude to the role of the accounting profession. Two alternative approaches which could characterize government attitudes are the interventionist and the *lassez-faire* approaches. Both may involve more regulation in the future, because of increasing complexity in the business and financial environment and changes in societal expectations, but the sources and means of regulation could be very different. A *laissez-faire* approach might place emphasis on private or professional regulation; for example the Securities and Investment Board has been established as a private body but with statutory backing. An interventionist approach would place more emphasis on the use of state agencies in regulation. Specific requirements associated with the reserved functions could also change, for example through changing the scope of the general audit requirement or increasing the types of external financial assessments to which companies are subject.

The Demands of Business

A further important factor in the development of the accounting profession has been its response to the demands of business. There are two aspects to this response: the supply of professional services to business, and the supply of suitable recruits for industrial and commercial management.

The accounting profession has provided the main source of supply for many general management positions, including senior executive positions, rather than being confined to a narrow 'accounting' domain in industry. In part this may be due to the absence of other significant competing sources of supply, such as are present in the United States, where graduates from business schools are relied upon in general management, or in continental Europe, where there is a tradition of teaching business economics in universities, which is seen as essentially distinct from accounting. However, the position of accountants in general management also reflects the ability of the accounting profession to see 'accounting' largely in terms of what its members do and not as limited by a single set of clearly defined functional activities.

This ability is also evidenced in the fact that accountants in public practice have been quick to identify growth opportunities and have responded to the demands of business and others for new services. Most recently, evidence of this trend is provided by the degree to which accounting firms have moved into areas of business consultancy, good examples being the fields of information systems and information technology and value-for-money work in the public sector.

In looking to the future, a number of alternatives may be postulated regarding the relationship between the accounting profession and the business community. First, there is a question as to whether the accounting profession will maintain or will lose its position as the premier supplier of recruits to business management. As long as the profession continues to recruit large numbers of the better graduates, then business will still be interested in subsequent recruitment, but this may not be a function of any enhancement gained while training as an accountant and so could be more susceptible to challenge by other sources of supply for management. Table 2.2, which is taken from Chapter 6 which deals specifically with the future of the finance function in industry, illustrates the danger of accounting losing its relevance to general management.

Table 2.2 Aptitudes and attitudes contrasted

Type F (finance)	Type A (accounting)
Business reality	Accounting convention
'Ball park' figures	Illusion of accuracy
Numbers last	Numbers first
Physical measures	Financial results
Measured risk-taking	Risk avoiding
Proactive	Reactive

As regards the nature of the services provided by professional firms, 'accounting' may continue to develop along the business consultancy route with a consequent diminution in the role of those activities associated with independent assessment and reserved functions, or, alternatively, the primary role of these latter activities may be maintained. These two possibilities have been described as illustrating two diverging 'cultures' of firms: those that will become 'conglomerates', continually diversifying into new services and areas of expertise, recruiting outside accountancy and becoming distant from the traditional professional base; and those that will continue to centre on services which are based on independent assessment.

The Flexibility of the Profession

It is clear from much of the above discussion that one of the most historically significant characteristics of accounting has been the fact that it has continually changed in terms of those activities which comprise 'accounting'. This fact reflects the flexibility and adaptability of the accounting profession, which can be seen in a number of different ways as follows:

1. Flexibility of domain. The accounting profession has expanded its domain as accountants have moved into a variety of positions in business and in the public sector.
2. Flexibility of services. The profession has adapted quickly to demands for new services, for example in a willingness to 'buy' in expertise not already present in firms.
3. Flexibility of knowledge base. Associated with the above has been the adaptability of the knowledge base associated with becoming an accountant. To some extent this adaptability can be seen in the coverage of the examination syllabus.

The nature of accounting and the role of the accounting profession in the future may depend on whether or not the above flexibility can be retained. Equally, the pressure for increasing diversity of activity may incur certain dangers, in that there may be limits to the amount of diversity of service and function which can be included within the boundaries of accounting as a single professional grouping. Overall, the skill set associated with chartered accountancy will be an important factor in exploiting future opportunities.

Reputation for Objectivity

A further factor which, it can be argued, has influenced the development of accounting in the past has been the reputation of the accounting profession for objectivity. This reputation is something which the profession has traded upon. It has been important to many of the activities which accountants have been involved in. For example, in external financial reporting, the independence of the auditor is implicit to the nature of the audit and the profession's role in regulating reporting practice can be seen as a function of this perceived quality. Equally, in insolvency and receivership, the accountant has exercised a role as an independent outsider coming in to act in the interests of affected parties, and in taxation work the objectivity of the accountant may be regarded as important by the Inland Revenue. Even in the area of business consultancy much of the profession's ability to obtain this type of work may derive from its reputation for objectivity and association with activities involving independent assessment.

The importance of this factor is also evidenced by the fact that the most significant structural changes in the accounting profession in recent years, for example the creation of the Accounting Standards Committee, the Auditing Practices Committee and the Joint Disciplinary Scheme, have been associated with periods when the profession's reputation for independent assessment has been subject to criticism. When this reputation has been threatened the profession has acted to protect it because of its centrality to the opportunities available to the members of the profession.

Constructing Scenarios

On the basis of the above discussion, a number of uncertainties can be listed, together with some factors which appear to be largely predetermined. These factors are summarized in Table 2.3. Making different assumptions about the uncertainties gives a basis for constructing the scenarios.

The Scenarios

Scenario 1

The first scenario is one based largely on the continuance of trends which are observable in the current environment. This scenario has two important roles in the analysis:

1. It allows consideration of the implications and interactions of some of the predictions which are commonly made concerning future developments in accounting.
2. It provides a benchmark against which the significance of changing certain assumptions in order to construct the other scenarios may be evaluated.

The Scenario
The UK economy develops in line with the trends experienced in recent years. The shift from manufacturing to services continues but the relative sizes of these sectors means that services do not provide sufficient compensation to give significant overall growth. National

economic growth continues to be slightly worse than international growth, and as the 1990s develop, inflation remains low and unemployment increases to four million. Opportunities and earnings in services increase but opportunities in manufacturing become relatively restricted and relative earnings are maintained principally

---

Table 2.3 Uncertain and predetermined components for constructing scenarios

---

UNCERTAINTIES

Economic growth	The rate of growth in the economy
Financial markets	The role of the City and the UK financial markets in an environment of increasing international competition
Reserved functions	The development of, and reliance upon, the 'reserved' functions by the state
Regulation	The extent to which the regulatory environment is one which restricts government involvement or is interventionist
Reputation for objectivity	The ability of the profession to maintain this reputation
Business recruitment	The extent to which the profession remains a major source of recruitment to business management
Growth opportunities	The relative importance to the professional firms of business consultancy services and services involving independent assessment

| Skill set | The extent to which the skill set of accountants develops in response to the demands of the environment |

PREDETERMINEDS

Internationalization	Markets will be increasingly international rather than national
Emphasis on services	The shift from manufacturing to services will continue
Skills	The skills demanded in the business environment will become increasingly specialized
Information technology	The potential availability of information will expand, and there will be a shortage of people to manage the technology and the information itself

---

through productivity. The role of the City and financial services remain important, particularly in the face of increasing internationalization.

The government is taken as committed to a *laissez faire* approach to regulation. Changes in the structure of the regulatory regime therefore concentrate on the framework of regulation rather than detailed rules and codes, reliance is placed on private sector regulation, and much is made of the notion of deregulation, partly through 'privatization' of regulatory mechanisms. Incorporation of practices also becomes possible.

The growth opportunities for professional firms remain more buoyant in the area of consultancy than in state mandated assessment activities. The profession also remains a principal source of supply of recruitment into industry and commerce but, with a wider range of skills being demanded, there is growing pressure on the traditional link between business requirements and the skills acquired and examined in a chartered accountant's training.

Analysis and Implications
In identifying the significant considerations arising out of this scenario, it is perhaps helpful to ask what is the limiting factor to the

growth of the profession and maintenance of opportunities for accountants? The main constraint would appear to be whether accountants will posssess the necessary skills to provide the consultancy services demanded and to match the type of skills business wants to recruit.

The growth opportunities for professional firms depend upon the possession of skills to satisfy the consultancy assignments available. In the short term, this need can be met by buying in the necessary 'non-accounting' expertise, or by retraining. For some firms, this position already exists. In the longer term the profession can attempt to cope with the expansion in the skill base by redefining the boundaries of the core knowledge required to be an accountant in order to include new skills. One of the main pressures on skills will be from information technology and its impact on the nature of transactions, finance and periodic reporting.

This latter strategy may also be necessary to maintain the relevance of chartered accountancy to industry and commerce. If chartered accountancy remains linked solely to the traditional skills, then relevance will decline. The professional firms may remain a source of recruits to business but this will be more as a function of qualifications gained by experience on consultancy assignments than by the professional qualification *per se*. The attractiveness of accountancy to graduate recruits may decline if there is a significant shift in industry's demand for qualified accountants, although this will also depend on the alternative sources of employment open to graduates. Indeed, professional firms could remain a significant path for graduates coming into industry, but without taking a professional qualification on the way if that qualification is not linked to the required skills.

In this world the larger professional firms will be consultancy growth oriented. They will recruit where necessary and will have an ever increasing recruitment which is not directly linked to the traditional professional bodies. The role of traditional skills will decline and there will be pressure within firms for auditors to be 'multifunction'. The staffing structures of the firms will change, with a smaller proportion being recruited as trainee accountants and a greater specialist staff. The value and significance of being a firm of 'chartered accountants' may be reassessed. With lower relative growth in the audit services market, competition will increase, with challenges to audit fees and increased pressure to accommodate clients' wishes.

For the smaller firm, the ability to buy in the necessary range of expertise will be less and the firms may therefore be faced with a choice between two strategies. They may either rely upon the traditional areas of work and settle for lower growth, attempt to improve efficiency and develop close relationships with clients, or they may attempt to become specialist consultancies. There will remain some middle ground where firms will be able to provide some general consultancy in association with the traditional functions but these will not be high growth areas.

As regards industry, chartered accountant recruitment will decline but this will be a slow process and the influence of accountants in industry will reduce only gradually. Industry will still recruit chartered accountants because of the available pool of quality staff, but again this may decline given changes within professional firms' staffing and recruitment. Non-accountants from professional firms will be as likely to be recruited by industry as will the chartered accountants.

From the point of view of the professional body the pressure will be to retain relevance to the activities of members. This pressure is likely to be greatest with respect to larger firms and industrial members. Relevance can be maintained by attempting to regulate or issue guidance on an increasing variety of subjects and by examining in these subject areas. It is questionable if the former strategy will be successful without the latter, i.e. will guidance be regarded as authoritative if the subject area is outside the core of accounting knowledge? If the variety of subject areas becomes too diverse it may be that the only way to maintain the relevance of the professional body will be through structural change with specialist divisions. The possible polarization between different types of practising firms and between practising and non-practising members will have to be reconciled in Institute policy.

Scenario 2

One of the most important factors in determining the development and role of accountancy is the regulatory regime and the relationship between the profession and the state. There are various pressures on this relationship, including the role of European legislation and public interest in the regulation of financial markets. Taking the first scenario and changing the assumption regarding the regulatory regime results in the following picture.

The Scenario
As in the first scenario, economic performance maintains the position reflected in current trends, i.e. relatively low growth, declining manufacturing, low inflation and high unemployment. The financial sector remains buoyant.

The major growth opportunities for professional firms are found outside the traditional reserved functions, with the associated recruitment and other considerations.

There is an interventionist regulatory regime. Significant importance is attached to those services which are linked to state mandated activities and involve independent assessment. The reputation of the profession as able and suitable to provide these services is not jeopardized by any specific problem events, but the sensitivity of government to the qualification of the profession is much higher than under a *laissez faire* regime. Emphasis is placed on the codification of rules surrounding the state mandated activities. Areas of professional self-regulation are seen more as matters of public policy and less as matters of private professional interest.

Analysis and Implications

As much of this scenario is the same as that of Scenario 1, it follows that much of the analysis will also be the same, for example the implications for firms wishing to pursue available growth opportunities and the need for chartered accountancy to be linked to skills which will maintain the opportunities for accountants. The changes in this scenario have to do with the visibility of the profession and the attitude of regulators, not the underlying economic variables. The main question is what difference does the change in the regulatory regime make?

The principal interaction of the assumption of an interventionist regime with the rest of the scenario would appear to be the relationship between the demands of the state and opportunities provided by industry and commerce. If the former places emphasis on traditional roles of independent assessment and the latter requires an ever increasing diversity of skills and services, is there a point at which these pressures come into conflict? The profession has had to consider this issue already in the context of the Eighth EEC Directive.

This issue raises interesting questions concerning the relationship between independent assessment, notably auditing, and consultancy services. If an interventionist regime placed strict standards on the importance of the independent assessment, would the potential conflict between this role and the provision of consultancy services become an issue? If the growth opportunities in consultancy are high, then it could be assumed that professional firms would be willing to sacrifice audit business rather than consultancy business; but is this really the case? How far does the consultancy work depend upon the association with independent assessment? Equally, to what extent is independent assessment enhanced because of the knowledge and information gained through consultancy activities?

At the very least, the professional bodies would have to continue
to address the question of the importance of state mandated work to
their members. This question goes beyond merely asking how much
of members' income is derived directly from state mandated
activities. It also has to do with a much more central issue of the role
of the relationship with the state in defining the status of the
accounting profession. Is it important to retain certain reserved
functions within the exclusive domain of accountants in order to
preserve the status of the profession; and do those reserved functions
therefore have significance beyond being part of a range of services?

Given an interventionist regime, the importance of the profession's activities to regulate in relevant areas will rise. The profession
will have to invest in its own regulatory processes in order to
preserve the impression of being capable of undertaking the reserved
functions. For example, the role of accounting standards and their
enforcement could be an increasingly important element in the
relationship between the profession and the state. This could also
apply to other areas of professional regulation. At present, the
Institute regulates technical matters, through accounting and
auditing standards, and professional conduct. The regulation of
professional conduct will include more active concern over compliance with technical standards.

In short, under Scenario 2, maintaining the opportunities for
accountants to the full would appear to be dependent on either (a)
persuading the state that there is no conflict between independent
assessment and the increasing diversification required to exploit
consultancy opportunities; or (b) investing in self-regulation to
ensure that it is perceived as preventing such conflict arising.

Scenario 3

Scenario 3 again takes the preceding scenario and builds upon it by
changing one part of the picture. One of the dominant elements in
the preceding two scenarios has been the availability of significant
growth opportunities for firms through consultancy services. Scenario
3 relaxes this assumption through introducing the possibility of more
problematic economic performance. This scenario attempts to
introduce a more radical discontinuity into the future, in the failure
of the UK financial markets, and the loss by the profession of its
reputation for objective judgement.

The Scenario

In this scenario it is assumed that even moderate economic growth
is not achieved. The trend in manufacturing remains as in previous

scenarios but the opportunities in services, and in particular the financial sector, are less optimistic. In the medium term, following deregulation, the City fails to meet the competition from international markets. There is an associated slump in the opportunities for accounting firms and also for individuals as the recent rise in professional salaries, driven by the financial services sector, is halted.

The problems in the financial markets are accompanied by failures of individual companies within those markets. These failures give rise to threats to the reputation and image of the accountancy profession. As the regulatory system is interventionist, the problems described above are likely to be accompanied by government investigation and action. Individual cases of alleged failures by professional firms place the profession on the defensive vis á vis the demands of an interventionist government.

Analysis and Implications
The first implication of this scenario is perhaps an unexpected one. In the previous two scenarios, industry's demand for an increasing variety of skills was accompanied by a similar demand within professional firms due to the availability of consultancy opportunities, and the question was how the accountancy profession could maintain relevance to these skills. In the present scenario, however, the demands of industry are not matched by a similar demand within firms, as the consultancy opportunities are not present. The likely implication of this is that the process of industry regarding the accountancy profession as a less suitable source of recruits for general management will be accelerated. In the short term, chartered accountants will still be well represented in general management, but in the medium term this position will deteriorate considerably. The profession will become more specialized in certain narrow areas and there will be an increased dependence on the state mandated roles.

At this point the significance of the regulatory regime can be considered. As the regulatory regime is interventionist, then events which seriously damage the image of the accountancy profession could lead to major changes in the existing relationship between the profession and the state. In contrast to the attempts to privatize regulation referred to in Scenario 1 the likely outcome is that moves would be made to increase control over the activities that accountants perform for the state and the profession could lose some of its existing regulatory roles. The effect of such intervention on the future of the accounting profession would be considerable because of (a) the importance of state mandated activities in defining the status of the profession; and (b) the fact that in this scenario the opportunities in business consultancy are depressed.

The size and influence of the profession could not be expected to show any significant increase and could in fact decrease somewhat. In the previous scenarios, the size of the profession could be expected to grow or remain stable through the general buoyancy of opportunities available to firms who recruit students. If opportunities fall, recruitment will be cut back and the size of the profession will probably decline.

Synthesis and Critical Issues

Reviewing the three scenarios, which are summarized in Table 2.4, one has focussed attention on skills and opportunities, one on the state and expectations, and one on economic failure. Having described a variety of possible futures, rather than attempting to pick one as the 'most likely', it is important to take the critical variables which the scenarios have identified collectively and consider these in the context of strategic planning. Drawing together the discussion it appears that a small number of critical points emerge. The principal interactions are between the relationship of the profession with the state and the relationship with business (the correspondence between the services and skills demanded and the abilities of the profession), as shown in Table 2.5.

Combination A would result in a continued shift of emphasis away from the traditional skills towards a wider diversity of services and skills.

Combination B would require a balancing in order to satisfy the demands of the business community and those associated with state mandated services.

Combination C could result in a reduction in the size of the profession, as well as its role and status, as opportunities are restricted.

Combination D implies a return to the emphasis on traditional skills and the importance of self-regulation.

The analysis may be followed through to consider areas of strategic decision making for the profession. The scenarios that have been described are based on various assumptions about environmental variables. The position of the accounting profession within any environment will also depend on organizational variables, that is,

TABLE 2.4 Summaries of Accounting Scenarios

SCENARIO 1	SCENARIO 2	SCENARIO 3
THE ECONOMIC ENVIRONMENT		
Economic growth positive but low	Economic growth positive but low	*Nil economic growth
Inflation low / Unemployment high	Inflation low / Unemployment high	*Inflation and unemployment rising
Relative importance of the financial sector high	Relative importance of the financial sector high	*Failure in financial markets
Opportunities and earnings greatest in services and high technology industries	Opportunities and earnings greatest in services and high technology industries	*Failure in areas of high technology
		*Financial failures have implications for reputation of the profession
THE REGULATORY ENVIRONMENT		
Emphasis on self-regulation and deregulation	*Emphasis on codification of rules	Emphasis on codification of rules
Legal changes concentrate on framework rather than detailed rules	*Reserved functions regarded as of major importance	Reserved functions regarded as of major importance
		*Expansion of state mandated assessments
BUSINESS SERVICES AND THE PROFESSION		
Consultancy opportunities higher than opportunities in reserved activities	Consultancy opportunities higher than opportunities in reserved activities	*Consultancy opportunities more limited
	*High visibility of reserved activities	*Recruitment opportunities in financial sector more limited
Wide range of skills demanded	Wide range of skills demanded	Wide range of skills demands
Industrial recruitment from profession maintained	Industrial recruitment from profession maintained	*Increased relative importance of traditional services and state mandated work
Increasing strain between business needs and professional skills	Increasing strain between business needs and professional skills	

* Components which have changed in comparison to the preceding scenario.

Table 2.5 Critical variables

The services demanded by business	Relationship with the state regulatory regime	
	Laissez faire	Interventionist
	Low emphasis on state mandated roles	High emphasis on state mandated roles
Consultancy opportunities and emphasis high	A	B
Consultancy opportunities and emphasis low	C	D

the things that are within the control of the profession and its members. Strategic decision making involves choices about these organizational variables. Although this chapter is not intended to make specific policy recommendations for any particular grouping, some comments will be made regarding use of the scenarios in strategic planning in the profession, referring back to the steps listed in part B of Figure 2.1.

In order to allow scenario analysis to have an impact on strategic decision making it is necessary to specify long term objectives to be pursued. These will vary between organizations and individuals but here a general objective for the accounting profession can be taken as maintaining and enhancing the position of members of the profession to exploit opportunities for employment, both individually and collectively.

A number of different general approaches could be adopted in pursuing this objective. One typology from the management literature distinguishes the three following types of strategic approaches (Miles and Snow, 1978):

1. Defenders. The main emphasis in the strategy of defenders is the protection of existing markets. Thus, policy is geared to

sealing off existing markets, and to increasing profitability through market share and efficiency. In terms of Table 2.4 this approach pays most attention to the horizontal axis. The risk of this strategy is that of not being able to respond to a major shift in the environment.

2. Prospectors. In contrast, prospectors emphasize the discovery and exploitation of new markets to maintain growth and profitability. Organizational policy is therefore geared to maintaining sufficient flexibility to identify and adapt to new opportunities. This approach would pay most attention to the vertical axis in Table 2.4. The risk of this strategy is of pursuing unsuccessful innovations, and of over-extending resources.

3. Analysers. Analysers seek to combine both of the above, by attempting to exploit new opportunities at the same time as maintaining a traditional core. Successful innovations will be adopted only when proved elsewhere. This description may be most descriptive of the accounting profession in the past. For a professional body, it may be difficult to follow any strategy other than this.

There is no single 'best' choice between the above strategies; each carries its own profile of possible risks and rewards. The choice will depend on the organization's objectives and its ability to exploit available opportunities.

The ability of members of the profession to benefit from the available opportunities chiefly depends upon the relevance of the skill set possessed by accountants to those opportunities, and the status of the qualification associated with membership of the profession.

These qualities are influenced by a number of factors, including the skills which are examined and therefore 'proved' in becoming an accountant, and the skills acquired by experience regarded as common to members of the profession. Reputational factors will also be important, both those relating to individual organizations and those deriving more generally from the role of the profession in regulating, and therefore standing as an authority, in certain areas of activity, and the association between the profession and certain state mandated activities.

Finally, it is necessary to identify the areas of strategy where decisions taken by the profession can influence these factors. These areas should be determined for each individual organization or interest group seeking to consider its strategy and policy. For the purposes of this chapter, two illustrative lists of areas of strategic decision making have been drawn up, one with reference to a professional body, and the other for an individual member or professional firm.

Professional bodies

Examples of the general strategic considerations to be addressed by a professional body are as follows:

1. Attempted sphere of influence. This is the only way that a professional body can remain important by staying in a narrow technical area and seeking to dominate and preserve authority in that area, or is the status of membership of the profession dependent on pursuing an authoritative position over an increasing sphere of influence? Are there any potential conflicts between different desired spheres of influence?
2. How is the sphere of influence to be maintained? This question involves issues to do with education (3), structure (4) and regulatory activity (5).
3. Education. To what extent is the perceived relevance of the skill set acquired by accountants dependent on those skills being proved through examination and thus being treated implicitly as part of the core knowledge of accountants?
4. Structure. Is it possible for the accounting profession to retain its relationship with an increasingly diverse set of activities within existing structures? Will increasing diversity in activities and skills force fragmentation of the profession and a narrowing of the sphere of influence?
5. Regulatory activity. How important are regulatory activities and standards of professional behaviour in maintaining the status of membership of the profession?

Individual members of the profession and firms

Examples of the strategic decisions of individuals and firms which the scenarios can contribute to are as follows:

1. Range of services. What range of services and 'image' is to be pursued by the firm (or for an individual what set of skills must be acquired to take advantage of available opportunities)?
2. Recruitment. What policy should be adopted towards the role of professional qualification in recruitment, in recruiting both expertise at a senior level and also more junior levels of staff?

Will those recruited in association with a professional accounting qualification be a decreasing proportion of staff?
3. Training. What are the implications of staffing policies and the range of services provided for training requirements within a firm or, for an individual, in addition to a professional qualification?
4. Size. What size of unit is necessary to be best placed to take advantage of the available opportunities?
5. Identity with the profession. To what extent will the title of 'chartered accountant(s)' remain an important asset in trying to exploit particular markets or job opportunities.

The result of the analysis in this chapter suggests that in each of the areas of strategic decision making, the alternative competing strategies should be evaluated against the two principal factors of the demands of business and the relationship between the profession and the state and their interrelationship.

Summary

The purpose of this chapter has been largely experimental, to explore the use of scenario planning in the context of the accounting profession as a means of assisting members of the profession to consider significant issues regarding the future. Three illustrative scenarios have been constructed, based on an analysis of significant factors which have influenced the role and development of accounting in the past and are likely to do so in the future. These scenarios have not been over-complicated and in many ways are closely related. The analysis has followed a pattern of changing assumptions gradually, rather than assuming three worlds which are all radically different from each other.

The outcome of the analysis may be considered with reference to the framework set out in Figure 2.1 to represent the role of scenario analysis in strategic decision making. The paper has concentrated mainly on area (A). It has identified two key variables.

First the response of the profession to demands from business regarding the services and set of skills required will critically affect the opportunities available to members of the profession.

Second the relationship between the profession and the state, will determine the opportunities in state mandated activities, the profession's role as a regulatory authority, and the status of the profession which in turn affects opportunities available to members.

Strategic decisions should therefore be evaluated against those two key factors. In this chapter, no attempt has been made to document specific strategies for evaluation (part B of Figure 2.1), but a number of key areas of strategy have been identified. They are as follows:

(a) levels and standards of recruitment to the profession;
(b) education and training requirements and the relevance to business of professional education;
(c) the range and development of services that can be encompassed within a single professional grouping;
(d) the structure of the professional bodies;
(e) the role of structures for self-regulation, and the importance of these structures and the associated rules in relation to state mandated activities;
(f) the growth or otherwise in the size of the profession.

It is hoped that the chapter thus provides a basis for individual decision makers to use in specifying explicit strategy alternatives and then to go on to make actual planning decisions (part C of Figure 2.1), whether these be at the level of a committee in a professional body, or an individual firm, or a grouping of members of the profession with common interests.

References

Drucker, P. (1985), *Innovation and Entrepreneurship*, Heinemann.

Leemhuis, J. (1985), 'Using scenarios to develop strategies', *Long Range Planning*, April 1985.

Lorenz, C. (1980), 'How Shell made its managers think the unthinkable', *Financial Times*, 5 March 1980.

Miles, R.E. and C.C. Snow (1978), 'Organizational strategy, structure and process', *Academy of Management Review*, July 1978.

Sims, D. and C. Eden (1984), 'Futures research: working with management teams', *Long Range Planning*, August 1984.

Wack, P. (1985), 'Scenarios: uncharted waters ahead', *Harvard Business Review*, September 1985.

PART TWO

Major Components of The Accounting Environment

3

Accountancy and the Development of the UK Economy

Accounting is, has been, and no doubt will continue to be, intimately involved with the development of the economy as a whole. As one of the most important forms of operational economic calculation, accounting has not only reflected prevailing economic conditions but has also played a significant role in enabling the implementation of different strategies for the management of both the national economy and particular enterprises within it.

Such an intertwining is reflected in the historical development of the accounting profession. The Great Depression at the end of the nineteenth century provided the basis on which the significance of a professionalized craft of economic calculation came to be recognized. Similarly, many of the origins of cost accounting can be traced to the economic requirements of the Great War; and the acquisition by accountants of the skills of financial management seems to have evolved from their involvement with distressed companies during the 1930s.

In more recent times the relationship between the economy and the development of accounting is also evident. The merger boom of the 1960s resulted in an enhanced public awareness of the role of reliable accounting reports. Inflation and the perceived need for a more informed incomes policy both had important consequences for accounting in the 1970s. More recently, the recession of the early 1980s provided an incentive for a greater diffusion of accounting skills into sectors of the economy which had not been so accustomed to the rigours of financial management. And changing conceptions of the economic role of the state, even now, are resulting in an expansion of the accounting domain and calls for new types of accounting expertise. One has only to observe the extensive change in the nature of the business of the large accounting firms to realize how significant the latter changes have been already.

Being so aware of the close intermingling of the problems of the economy and accountancy, the Understanding a Changing Environment Group sought to explore the economic future and the implications that this might have for accounting policy making.

The Economic Past

Any analysis of probable economic futures must be based on our past experiences. Only by forming judgements about the causes of our past and present economic performance can we gain an insight into what the future may hold in store for us.

The economic experience of the United Kingdom in the last hundred years can be divided into four periods of alternating good and bad times.

1. *Up to 1914*
    In this period Britain was a great trading nation. Much of the nation enjoyed increasing prosperity. That prosperity was built, however, not on prowess in manufacturing, as is often suggested, but upon income from the nation's many foreign investments, colonies and possessions.

2. *The Inter-War Years*
    Between the wars the United Kingdom, along with the rest of the developed world, experienced a long period of depression. There was a decline in prices as the country pursued a tight monetary policy. For the United Kingdom, this was a period of relative as well as absolute decline because much of the country's foreign wealth had been expended in the 1914—18 War. The Second World War would disperse this wealth still further. In the latter part of the period, however, growth picked up, fuelled considerably by the rearmament programme.

3. *1945 to 1973*
    A long period of prosperity for the developed world followed the Second World War. The prime cause of this seems to have been the ordered growth of the international economy, brought about by the Bretton Woods agreement. The dollar was tied to gold and everything else was tied to the dollar. The United States adopted conservative monetary policies, yet the rest of the world

was 'hungry for dollars'. The United States was able to run a continuing small deficit in trade, in the process stimulating the international economy. Other important factors behind the post-War period of growth included the need for the countries of Western Europe to repair the damage of the War and the scope that they enjoyed to catch up with economic advances that had been made in the United States; an abundance of cheap raw materials and fuel; and the growth of international trade fostered by GATT and the Kennedy round.

4. *1973 to the present*
The post-War prosperity contained the seeds of its own destruction. Although the oil price shocks of 1974 and 1979 are often identified as a major reason for the era of low growth (on average less than half that of the previous period) we have experienced subsequently, other factors too were at work. The growth of other economies had produced a relative weakening of the dominance of the United States and the strength of the dollar. The continuing US trade deficit and the costs of the Vietnam War, which were financed by the printing of dollars, created a climate in which such factors as an unprecedented rise in commodity prices, the end of the 'catch up' period in which European prosperity emerged after post-War reconstruction, the emergence of protectionist inclinations, and the 1974 oil price shock, led to deflation. Governments are now pursuing restrictive policies and reducing expenditures. Monetary control has been widely emphasized. There has been a rise in unemployment nearly everywhere.

In retrospect, the general trend of post-War prosperity and its relative decline seems to have had little to do with the policies pursued by specific national governments, with the possible exception of the United States. The primary factors at work seem to have been international in character — commodity prices, exchange rates, tariff reductions and technical advance. Similarly, the major economic problem now facing governments is also international: unemployment is at high levels in the developed Western economies. However, the international factors lying behind such general trends do not deny that specific national environments and governments can have an effect. Indeed, distinct differences seem to be observable: the United States and Japan have so far been able to create new jobs, whereas Europe has been comparatively less successful. For many Europeans, therefore, the key economic issues for the medium term relate to the causes of unemployment and its remedy.

The Economic Future

The failure to maintain economic growth and full employment has resulted in a division on macro-economic theory among economists. Twenty-five years ago there was no doubt that Keynesian theories were dominant. That consensus has now been shattered. Be that as it may, there nevertheless seems to be agreement about at least some of the main factors which will determine economic performance over the next fifteen years. These are as follows:

1. The structure of the developed economies. Everywhere, except in the Far East, manufacturing is in relative decline. This has been the cause of considerable concern to some, but an alternative view is that jobs in the service sector are no less valuable than jobs in manufacturing. It is perhaps worth noting that despite the recent precipitous decline, 32 per cent of jobs in the private sector in the United Kingdom are still in manufacturing, whereas in the United States the comparative figure is 25 per cent. Nevertheless, because of the continuing growth of trade at a rate which has been roughly twice that of economic growth, the importance of manufactured goods should not be underestimated. The United Kingdom is highly dependent on trade and it is difficult to envisage a growth in internationally traded services which will parallel the rise in the volume of manufactured imports.

2. The United States remains the dominant world economy. Although at the time of the Group's meeting this was expressed in terms of strong performance of the US economy and the associated rise in the dollar confirming this, it was noted that the dollar seemed over-valued and could fall very quickly. Subsequent events have reinforced such a view. The attitude taken by the United States towards deficit spending must be an important factor in economic growth worldwide, and defence expenditures are a major component of that spending. Another key US policy variable is the stance taken towards free trade. A shift towards protectionism would have a very serious impact upon the international economy. It is difficult to see how international prosperity could grow, were the United States to turn its back on the free trade system, and there are some signs that this might be a real possibility.

3. The shift of economic activity to the Pacific Basin has major implications for European economies. While industrial growth

in the region increases competition for European manufactured goods and there is a danger that Europe will come to be seen as very distant from the Far East—United States economic axis, economic growth in the region also provides new markets and new opportunities for prosperity in which Europe may be able to share.

4. The development of the financial system. The international exchange market has been largely privatized. Up until the early 1970s, most international liquidity was controlled by governments. Now the majority of transactions are between banks. There is a huge volume of lending by banks to developing countries, much of which looks precarious at high levels of interest rates, and where individual banks have no effective sanctions against their creditors. While the system may not collapse, a return to the order and discipline of a system similar to Bretton Woods seems unlikely. However, greater stability for the pound would ensue if it were to be brought within the European Monetary System.

What does this analysis imply for the future of the UK economy? It seems that prospects for the world economy are no more than moderate; they may be poor. Given that the United Kingdom has in the past under-performed in relation to its competitors, it seems that the best to be expected is that the United Kingdom could perform, on average, as well as other nations. But there are some negative factors to be faced. Oil revenues will decline as North Sea production passes its peak and the UK manufacturing sector, which still needs to provide the main component of trade, seems relatively weak. Thus the two economic scenarios at the extremes of reasonable feasibility seem to be as follows:

1. Moderate international growth and moderate UK performance. The world economy might grow at, say, 3 per cent, with the UK economy growing at 3 per cent along with it.

2. Poor international growth and poor UK performance. The world economy might grow at only 1—2 per cent and the UK economy would have nil growth.

A 3 per cent growth rate would suggest that the United Kingdom might maintain unemployment at more or less present levels until well into the 1990s. A nil growth rate would mean that unemployment continued to rise.

Some Implications for Accountancy

Is it possible to derive from such economic prospects any implications of importance to accountants? All too clearly this is a hazardous task, but the Group did identify a number of significant themes.

With economic restraint continuing, careful financial management and finely tuned economic calculation are likely to remain the order of the day. In this respect, consideration needs to be given to the implications for the profession and the accounting body of knowledge of the division of the economy among services, the public sector and manufacturing industry. A continuing relative decline in manufacturing may mean traditional management accounting skills will need to be re-evaluated. These factors, together with the growth of flexible manufacturing systems and continuing inroads by information technologies into the accountant's role as provider of internal management information, will mean that management accountants will need to become expert in new areas of knowledge if their craft is not to decline. The diffusion of accounting skills into new areas seems likely to continue, with its attendant implications for the financial control of different organizations having different economic structures. The exporting of services will become more important and this is an area where accountants may be called upon to make a new contribution. Financial services have become increasingly international. A demand for related work from accountants is likely to be the forerunner of a future expansion of invisible accounting exports. Although peculiarly sensitive to changes in political ideology and social expectations, accounting for and within the state nevertheless seems to be a topic of continuing concern. And a greater emphasis on the importance of maintaining competition, especially where technological change is very rapid, may imply new roles for accountants and new ways of controlling natural monopolies, such as has already been seen in the privatization of telephone services and gas supplies.

A continued internationalization of the economy is likely to place increased emphasis on international accounting and international accounting standards.

Because of the importance of the international economy, the success or otherwise of the financial services provided by the City may have a more than proportionate effect on the rest of the economy. In this context, the reforms of the financial services sector need to be evaluated carefully. A failure for measures of self-regulation might mean that a statutory basis for City regulation will become necessary. It is likely that fundamental changes to standard setting and the regulation of the accountancy profession would follow as a result.

Despite taking a cautious view of economic growth, the Understanding a Changing Environment Group identified the presence of powerful forces for change in the work of accountants. Although economics can give us only a partial view of the future, it can also point us to the likelihood of important social changes which can accompany economic trends. A nation with continuing high levels of unemployment is likely to find rapid changes in the nature of work and participation in the economy. It is therefore appropriate to follow an analysis of economic prospects by an examination of the changing society in which accounting will function.

4

Accountancy and Social Development in the United Kingdom

Like the recent history of the economy, our immediate experience of social development is one of relative disappointment and disillusion when compared with the optimism of the 1960s. There has been a widespread loss of faith in society's ability to control and improve both economic growth and the wellbeing of members of society. While diminution in the quality of life for many is clearly linked to poor economic performance — especially as experienced by, for example, the unemployed — there are additional factors affecting the social environment of which accounting is ultimately a product.

During the 1960s and early 1970s there seemed to be broad agreement that social spending on such matters as health, welfare, education, social security and unemployment benefit was just, worthwhile and, in the long run, economically beneficial. In any event, in a growing economy with full employment, social spending could be projected to fall as a proportion of national income, or if it did not, then the spending was widely regarded as a deliberate choice reflecting an intent to care for the disadvantaged. Subsequently, however, the consensus about social spending and the legitimate objectives to be pursued by social policy has to a certain extent broken down.

Social policy has now become an area subject to rational analysis, calculation and managerial tradeoff rather than the dictate of consensual politics. As a direct consequence, sections of the accountancy profession are becoming involved in numerous areas of social as well as economic concern. Already there are many examples of reports by firms of accountants (or consultants associated with them) on local authority services, the provision of social services and other related topics, which go beyond merely documenting financial implications and which address issues of social choice, even if they studiously avoid (and many would say rightly so) reaching definitive, explicitly valuebased conclusions. Even so, although accountants are still feeling their way in this type of work, there are some signs of a growing awareness of the implications that it might have for the maintenance of their perceived independence.

The low level of economic growth in nearly all developed countries since the mid1970s, with its attendant increase in unemployment, has polarized opinion. The ascendancy of marketbased and monetarist economic policies in some countries has been associated with an emphasis upon the moral value of selfreliance by members of society and concerted attempts to reduce social spending, or at least restrain the natural growth associated with increasing unemployment.

In the United Kingdom, the elimination of large income differentials and poverty — both in its economic and social senses — which was widely expected in the egalitarian 1960s, has been confounded by an observed deterioration in many social indicators. Crime continues to increase. The percentage of the population in receipt of supplementary benefits continues to rise. Regional differences — the north/south divide — are becoming more marked and we can see the emergence of new grey areas in our cities.

At the same time, the beneficiaries of much social support, notably higher education and mortgage tax relief, continue to be the middle classes rather than the poor, even if government expenditure on these items has been cut in real terms.

Such increases in social divisions have not happened only in the United Kingdom. The European Commission continues to report increases in the number of people living in poverty throughout Europe. There is widespread failure of social foresight worldwide, as evidenced by the failure in the developed world both to recognize the inevitability of the crises in Ethiopia and the Sahel, or to apply different prescriptions for the integration and overall assessment of the investment plans which are used to evaluate lending to third world countries. Although the cost of social policies in the United Kingdom and elsewhere in the developed world has been rising faster than gross domestic product (GDP), the United Kingdom has fallen behind in its social spending in comparison with other European states: within the EC, only Greece now spends less than the United Kingdom on social welfare as a percentage of GDP. At the same time, the United Kingdom is not highly taxed as a nation: again as a percentage of GDP, taxation in the United Kingdom is lower than in many of the other economically successful countries in Europe.

Social Prospects

Given this recent experience and without any prospect of rapid, sustained economic growth in the immediate future, it is difficult to be optimistic about social developments. It is difficult to envisage a society where there are significantly fewer poor, where there is less crime, and in which social inequalities are less important.

Economic and social divisions are widening across age bands of society. The young and the old tend to be more poorly off, to have worse living conditions and to live in more socially deprived areas than the relatively well-off group of people aged 45—60. Couples in this age group, whose children are more or less independent, and where there is a marked tendency for both partners to be in work, seem likely to be especially welloff. (It must be remembered that, although recent economic performance has been poor, growth in earnings has been running ahead of inflation so that real earnings have been increasing.)

Another factor of some significance is the growing internationalization of the economy, with multinational firms relocating employment to low cost labour countries in the third world. Manufacturing jobs in the United Kingdom have suffered as a result. When seen in such terms, the exporting of jobs may mean that poverty is being imported from the third world.

The Future of Work

The effects of social change are felt not only by the poor and the unemployed. Strong forces are affecting the type of work people do and the way in which they do it. Some important past trends can be expected to continue. Britain's productivity gains will continue to be moderate, the recent large gains having been a result of the onceandforall shake out in manufacturing. Unemployment will not fall much from its present level.

However, there have also been a number of important recent changes in the structure of employment, as follows:

1. The decimation of the manufacturing base of the economy, the increase in employment in service industries and a small shrinkage in the public sector has changed the mix of jobs.
2. Increasing manufacturing productivity has continued a wellestablished trend towards a predominantly white collar labour force; most people now work in offices rather than factories.

3. There has been a large shift of jobs to service industries in the south of England and away from the traditional manufacturing areas.
4. There are more women at work than previously; 43 per cent of the labour force is now female, probably now a stable proportion.
5. The labourforce is middle-aged; the falling birthrate and high youth unemployment means that the average age of the workforce is increasing.
6. There has been a trend towards parttime employment; 20 per cent of the workforce are part-timers.
7. There has been an upturn in selfemployment, now at its highest level since 1921.

There have also been changes in the structure of organizations. The size of the establishment in which work is carried out has tended to get smaller and companies have tended to subcontract the manufacturing of components and of other aspects of their business, rather than carry out such work inhouse. Federalism in companies has increased. Organizations have become decentralized and divisionalized; more operational authority has been given to divisional managements.

There has been a change in the pattern of work for employees, who recently could expect to work forty-eight hours of the week, forty-eight weeks of the year, for forty-eight years of their lives. Now workers can expect to spend longer in training, and thus make a late start in the job market, and they can expect to retire earlier. Working hours are decreasing and holidays and sickness entitlement increasing. A worker may now reasonably expect to work thirty-five hours a week, for thirty-five years; and not counting periods of leave and training, etc., a thirty-five week year is in sight.

There have been pervasive changes, too, in the management of industrial relations. Corporatism — the influence of government, TUC and the CBI and other employers' federations on industrial relations — has declined and a considerable structure of laws has replaced the previous voluntary framework of industrial bargaining. Although employers have made no concerted assault on the unions, management has shown a distinct tendency to reassert itself.

The personnel function within business seems to have become less important as line managers have been able to impose their preferences upon less militant workforces. There now seems to be less overt conflict in organizations and a greater interest in exploring new motivational and reward structures. As a result, the focus of the personnel function is moving from the management of industrial relations to what is now termed the management of the human resource. The consequent increase in personnel systems and procedures is already providing possibilities for a greater articulation with the financial systems operated by the accountant.

The level of bargaining in organizations also seems to have become more decentralized: there is less emphasis upon maintaining national agreements and more upon relating pay to local market conditions. One effect of this has been to deny unions a voice in strategic issues affecting an organization as a whole. For the accountant, bargaining at levels below that of the organization provides new problems in the provision of financial and other information. Where the reported profitability of a plant or a division relies on transfer pricing, the information which accountants will be asked to provide for use in pay negotiations will need to be carefully designed and prepared on an agreed basis.

Despite the widespread employer opposition to the implications of the Vredling proposals and the Bullock Report, more attention is at last being paid to joint consultation between management and workforce. Business and work councils are becoming increasingly common and there is much more information made available to workforces. However, it is an open question how permanent the shift of the 'frontier of control' in favour of management will be, if ever the external threat of unemployment is removed from industrial relations.

The power of trade unions has diminished and may continue to do so. In 1979, 55 per cent of the workforce was unionized. In the 1990s the level is likely to be 40—45 per cent . However, this proportion is still a high one by international standards and the unions are likely to continue to be a major factor in industrial relations. But the character of the unions can be expected to change because of several factors. These include: the influence of mergers between unions brought about by the decline in their membership; changes in the relative balance of power arising from shifts in patterns of employment; fragmentation of the workforce and, not least, the influence of legislation on union operation. The unions may also be less likely to align themselves uniformly with the Labour Party and may become more akin to pressure groups intent on attaining action on particular issues.

Unionization within accountancy practices still seems unlikely while opportunities for mobility upwards to partnership or outwards to industry and commerce remain. Even so, changes in technology and the task structure of the profession are likely to increase the number in clerical rather than technical positions — historically a trend with which the profession has been concerned. The professional accountancy bodies themselves, which in some senses (e.g. IMACE) operate as trade unions for their members, are likely to have a more difficult role with the growing diversity of interests stemming from changes taking place in both the structure of the profession and the tasks undertaken by it.

The Social Context

Accounting cannot function in isolation from the social context in which it operates. In the past, the rise of a political interest in institutional accountability provided the context for a vast expansion of the audit function in both the private and public sectors. The growth of the labour movement resulted in a greater awareness of the need to manage financial motivations for action within the enterprise. The development of the modern state gave rise to a vast increase in the amount and complexity of economic calculation undertaken in society. These and many other associated changes have resulted in the accountancy profession as we now know it.

Even in recent years social developments have had a profound impact on the profession. Together with the development of a more articulate publicly orientated financial media, demands for even greater institutional accountability have provided one of the important bases for the accounting standards project. Throughout its history the project has had to face the consequences of changing political ideologies, shifts in the power of the labour movement and, not least, a wider questioning of the bases of legitimacy for its own actions.

When seen in such terms, what might be some of the implications of possible future changes in the social domain? With the breakdown of consensus on social issues, a demand has grown for the increased accountability of many public sector organizations which are the vehicles of social policy. Accountants are already beginning to satisfy the demand for reports on the inputs to, and outputs from, such organizations, and such work is likely to continue and to increase. Furthermore, unless there is a radical shift in political preferences, we are likely to see a further increase in the development of managerial, rather than political, decision making in such organizations — a trend that will further increase the accountant's involvement.

Increased consultation at workplaces will bring demands for new types of information provision as employees and unions are included in a wider consultative process than traditional bargaining over pay and conditions. Society, however, is unlikely to become any less divided. Indeed, there may be a growing need for security and control over financial and physical assets and transactions.

5

The Future of the Professional Firm

'May you live in interesting times' is said to be an ancient Chinese curse and few accountancy practitioners will disagree, whatever size of firm they come from, that at present the professional firm of accountants is passing through 'interesting times'.

In this chapter the changing nature of the professional firm is investigated in order to identify the forces now at work which might predetermine the pattern of the future for the professional firm.

The discussion here is generalized across the range of firm size, from smaller practices to the largest. It might be expected that practitioners operating in different markets would be subject to significantly different forces affecting the future. In fact, a very similar range of unresolved issues are critical to the future of professional firms of differing sizes, although the manner in which these issues can or will be resolved might vary.

The Work of the Profession

Although the work of accountants has always evolved, over the past decade the speed of evolution has increased. The kinds of work which professional firms do and the relative importance of different aspects of that work are changing quite rapidly, as are the skills needed to carry it out.

There has been a fall in the relative importance of audit work, especially in larger firms, and a growth of new types of work, particularly in the public sector and in consulting. Moreover, the quantity of work available to the profession seems to be growing despite the economic and social scenarios described in earlier chapters. While growth potential might be restrained by a number of factors, availability of work is not one of them. For the present there seems to be no reason why the rate of change experienced in the past decade should slow down, and further shifts in the mix of work done by firms can be expected.

The External Environment

Previous chapters have identified a number of key forces, external to the profession, which determine the scenarios affecting all aspects of accounting, including the development of professional firms. The following factors are likely to be particularly important:

(a) the shift from manufacturing industry to service industry;
(b) the changing culture of organizations, typified by increasing federalism, divisionalization and autonomy;
(c) the move to the 'information age', where the processing, dissemination and use of information as a commercial activity is becoming increasingly important relative to the processing and handling of physical goods;
(d) the technological change in the manufacture and design of products and in the internal systems of organizations;
(e) the growth of information technology in processing business information.

The last three items are inter-related and based on the rapid development of computer technology; they imply an increasing need for specialization by practising accountants as the technological sophistication of their clients increases. The impact of computerization, and information technology in particular, is foreseen as such an important area of change that the Group devoted an entire meeting to the topic.

Despite the best efforts of the government, increasing fragmentation and specialization of business means that the complexity of regulation faced by businesses continues to increase. As a result, yet more specialization in accounting firms will ensue as firms equip themselves to assist clients in the compliance with new regulations. Other factors in the external environment have been dealt with in previous chapters and will not be repeated here.

Liability and Accountability

The recent marked tendency of aggrieved users of accounts to seek redress from firms of accountants will probably continue. It is unlikely that any government will find restrictions to the liability of professionals of sufficiently high priority to provide relief, even if governments could be persuaded of the merits of such a course.

Over the longer term greater concern with professional liability and the need to demonstrate independence could increase pressure for separating audit work from other areas of work. Moreover, if incorporation of auditing firms becomes possible, the professional bodies will need to provide regulations in a number of areas, for example: how widely ownership of the shares of such firms can be held; how management of audit companies will be arranged; and how discipline over companies will be enforced.

The Place of Audits in the Work of Firms

The post-War development of large firms of accountants has been dominated by the growth of the audit business. The growth arose principally because of the increasing concentration of industries in the United Kingdom as a result of the numerous mergers and takeovers which have taken place since 1945, and from the increasingly technical and rigorous nature of modern auditing. As the number of listed companies has declined because of mergers, so the average size of the companies making up the private sector has increased, providing both the need for larger auditing firms to service such clients and for increasingly sophisticated systems of auditing.

Although audit has never been one of the predominant services provided by smaller practitioners, the increased disclosure required by the Companies Act of 1967 for their limited company clients and the implementation of auditing standards by the professional bodies has increased the attention and the priority which such firms have had to give to audit work.

There is good reason to believe, however, that the predominance of auditing in the development of firms has ended. For smaller firms there is pressure to exempt small companies from audit requirements. Many smaller practitioners would welcome such a change; they believe that the removal of the compulsory audit would enable them to service clients more constructively, by releasing resources and by allowing them to become more involved with clients' business needs.

For larger firms there has been an explosion of non-audit work. And for them two distinct scenarios are beginning to appear. Firms may begin to divide between those firms for which auditing will remain the dominant culture, even if it is not the majority of their business, and firms for which auditing becomes just one of a wide range of services.

For audit-based firms the key services are likely to be based upon independence, which the firm will need to guard rigorously; the contribution to the control of organizations which the firm can provide; and the attest function of providing opinions and reports to third parties.

For the other firms ('conglomerate firms'), auditing may need to be separated from the dominant activities associated with the provision of a wide range of services. Such services are likely to centre on advising, and reporting on inherently uncertain and subjective topics, together with assistance in the implementation of new developments. Such firms' work will often be for the benefit of the management of their clients rather than for third parties.

In both these scenarios it is possible to see that it will be important to protect the firms' independence when conducting audit and similar work. In any case cross-subsidization where relatively cheap auditing leads to highly profitable consulting engagements has declined: large clients are no longer looking for 'one-stop shopping' for accounting and consulting services.

The growth in litigation is symptomatic of a growing perception of the auditor among the financial laity as, in some sense, a guarantor not only of the financial statements but also the financial condition of a company. Associated with this view is the perception that auditors should have some responsibility for the detection and reporting of fraud, particularly management fraud.

It seems unlikely that concern about fraud, particularly in financial organizations, will go away. Increased monitoring and control of financial organizations seems inevitable and there does not seem to be any potential provider of such services other than these organizations' auditors. The profession will have to come to grips with this and adopt a regulatory role with regard to financial fraud.

Almost inevitably this responsibility will lead to some breach of confidentiality between the client and the auditor but the profession will need to be prepared to confront this. In this respect auditing is likely to acquire a higher profile and become a riskier activity involving some very difficult judgments. As financial markets have become international, and ingenuity in creation of new financial instruments is apparently boundless, the appropriate validation and disclosure of transactions is becoming ever more contentious and difficult to determine.

Recruitment and Training

It is perhaps surprising that in a time of very high unemployment and when the rewards of accountants have been increasing much faster than average earnings, recruitment into the profession should present a problem. Yet, large firms spend enormous sums of money recruiting new students and small firms complain, constantly, of the difficulty of finding suitable staff. However, as 10 per cent of UK graduates going into employment now begin to train as chartered accountants, the size of the profession's demand for suitable manpower is already putting the available supply under some strain. Firms of all sizes seem to want more graduates as their businesses grow, and the demands of industry for graduates seem to be increasing as the recession abates. As, at the same time, the size of the teenage population is declining, no decrease in the scarcity of new entrants to the profession can be foreseen. Indeed, manpower may become the limiting factor which will inhibit growth in the profession. Since pressure for changes in the organization structures of firms is likely to arise as a result of other forces, shortage of professional grade staff may cause the growth of career grades at the non-qualified level.

The setting of standards for the education and training of accountants seems to be one area where professional bodies have a role which cannot be carried out by practising firms, however large they are.

The Role of the Professional Bodies

Apart from setting educational standards, what other roles can the Chartered Institutes and other professional bodies expect to carry out in future?   On the regulatory front there seem to be three possibilities as follows:

1. The Institutes' roles will expand to regulate the majority of activities of firms. For example, standards for work on consultancy engagements might be produced.
2. The Institutes will concentrate on maintaining professional standards for the core businesses of auditing, accounting and tax work, while allowing other businesses within firms to develop in an unregulated fashion.
3. The role of the Institutes will contract to become that of bodies providing an entrance-level qualification and little else.

Each of these possibilities has implications for the non-regulatory work of the Institutes, for example their representative roles and their members' services activities, which would tend to follow the pattern of the regulatory activities.

An extreme version of possibilities 1 or 3 above seems unlikely. It is difficult to see the influence of the Institutes extending far into the areas of business of firms where the majority of staff owe no allegiance to accountancy as their parent discipline, unless it becomes expedient for firms to demonstrate independent supervision of that kind of work. A series of major scandals caused by poor non-accounting work might produce a call for a much extended role for the Institutes, but the possibility seems remote.

Similarly, it is unlikely that the Institutes would be reduced to a rump, losing all their regulatory power, unless detailed regulation were taken over by the state; for there is no other possible provider of the service. Nevertheless, more state involvement is one eventuality which should be examined in some depth. In a mild form, it could lead to an increase in the authority of professional bodies.

At present, it does not seem likely that the 'frontier of regulation' will move to an extreme position, but it cannot be expected to remain static. Within bounds, quite rapid switches in the regulatory frontier can occur: for example, new forms of regulation may be imposed as a response to public demand, or the collapse of particular forms of authority may occur as support for them is withdrawn by the accounting community.

The Work of Smaller Practitioners

The problems facing smaller practitioners are, in many respects, similar to the problems of larger firms, but their responses may need to differ. There is a market niche for the small firm. Recently, competition in that niche from banks and the larger firms has been met; competition from those sources does not now seem a threat to them. If the compulsory audit for small firms is abolished, competition from unqualified practitioners may increase a little, but most smaller practitioners are confident that their services are of sufficient quality to overcome price competition from unqualified firms.

The most serious problems facing smaller practitioners are recruitment, specialization and information technology. Although smaller practitioners are adamant that 'quality of life' in a smaller firm exceeds that in larger firms, the cost of students and qualified staff is becoming prohibitive. The growth of specialized knowledge means that it is becoming ever more difficult for the general practitioner to keep up-to-date. And while information technology provides enormous potential for savings and for new services to clients, the cost, in terms of effort and of a continual adaption to changes in the technology, is enormous and erodes chargeable time.

These factors suggest that there is considerable evolutionary pressure on the smaller firm. We may expect to see development of specialization in certain roles, as is already occurring, for instance, in insolvency. Firms may separate into 'general practitioners' and 'consultants', with some large firms among the consultants. Loose federations of small firms will continue to develop along the lines of training consortia, but expanding into areas of specialization, recruitment and information technology. Information technology may allow other organizational changes to develop, which may cause an increase in the ratio of career-grade junior staff to senior staff. Amid this evolution one thing is certain: firms which do not adapt will cease to provide a reasonable living for their partners.

Summary — The Culture of Accounting

The changes described in this chapter have profound implications for the internal organization and culture of accounting firms. Is there a core of accounting which is relatively constant, or will firms become diffuse conglomerates with employees owing allegiance to a functional specialism or a divisional subunit rather than the common identity of accounting?

For some accountants the predominance of what they see as the central culture determines the organization of the firm. They see that the formula, 'Get the right people and train them well in the ways of the profession and the firm', has served them well in the past and they expect it to do so in the future.

For others, accounting is distinguished from other professions by its willingness to adapt and take on new, profitable roles. That is not to say that evolution is free or unguided, but it does imply a willingness to change organizational culture and structure rapidly and a faith that the unforeseen problems of change will somehow or other come right in the end.

There is probably a role for both types of firm, but their coexistence under the title of 'Chartered Accountants' is likely to provide problems of resolution and identity for the Institute as a whole.

6

The Future of the Accountant in Industry

It is a universally acknowledged truth that the financial director of a company should be a qualified accountant; or is it? About ten years ago a survey of the board membership of Britain's leading companies would have shown that in more than 90 per cent of cases the financial director of the company was a qualified accountant. However, this pattern is changing. An analysis of the companies in the *Times* 1000 companies today would probably show less than 70 per cent accountant financial directors. Even the 100 Group of financial *eminences grises* from major companies now includes non-accountants. It is entirely possible that the United Kingdom is moving towards the pattern of many other countries, for example the United States and Germany, where senior financial executives are recruited from a basis that is much wider than the accountancy profession. In the United States only about a quarter of financial vice presidents are CPAs, although that figure has been growing in recent years.

A number of factors are involved in the pre-eminence of accountants in the finance function in British industry. In its early days, it should be remembered that the profession would have little to do with being directly involved with 'trade'. The First World War started to change that, however. Even the most senior members of the profession became involved in the financial control of wartime contracting arrangements. Their role in cost and price control, and the investigation of accusations of war profiteering, not only provided a direct stimulus for the development of more sophisticated systems of cost control in British industry, but also an enhanced social respectability for the industrial accountant — a most important consideration in the British context. Working in industry started to become a little more OK.

From this foot-hold accountants moved into the niche created by the need for costing and management accounting information during the post-War industrial reconstruction. In time of social and political, as well as economic difficulty, accountants also came to play a number of important roles in mediating relationships between industry, the City, government and the labour movement.

No Competition

Although accountants have never become the dominant experts in financial institutions and the City, until recently there has been little competition from other disciplines for the role of financial decision makers in British industry and commerce. So a demand was established for a service for which there were few alternative sources of supply. The United Kingdom does not have a large output of trained and financially aware graduates from business schools, as does the United States. Nor does it have a tradition, like that of Germany (and many other countries in continental Europe), of producing applied business economists seeking employment in industry. In the United Kingdom education has tended to concentrate on academic virtues. Even in economics, theory has been emphasized over praxis or a more focused interlinking of theory with practice.

The result has been that anyone wanting financial expertise, or even applied economic skills (as evidenced by some of the developments in the public sector), has almost always had to turn to the accountancy profession.

That situation may now be changing, however. It is possible to discern that competition for the financial decision making role is beginning to arise. In a small number of companies, mainly, it must be admitted, American-based companies, finance and treasury departments are training bright graduates from scratch in a new tradition of financial management. In effect, these departments are becoming financial business schools and the people they train are disseminating this tradition as they move to influential positions in other companies. In addition, the graduates of business schools proper are now much more visible in senior financial and managerial positions.

Given that such developments are taking place, it is both interesting and important to inquire into how non-accountant finance directors view the role of financial decision makers in organizations, and how they see accountants as being able to contribute to this role.

Two Views

It is possible to contrast two views of the financial function which represent very different ways of integrating financial concerns into the wider organizational culture. One view (a 'Type A' approach) emphasizes an accounting outlook on the world and concentrates on the provision of conventional sources of information and compliance with legal and other regulatory requirements. According to an opposing view (the 'Type F' approach), the financial function is a more active, integral part of the management process. Existing primarily to contribute to the organizational decision making approach, it provides an influential economic language for decision making and a range of approaches for the more proactive management of the financial resources of an enterprise. From this latter viewpoint, accounting *per se* tends to be seen as a narrower area of technical expertise. 'Bean counting', 'margin-shaving' and 'internal audit' were the phrases that emerged in the discussion. The metaphor of the accountant as one who 'after the battle counts the dead and bayonets the wounded' was used to typify this view. Although few people would dispute that such control related functions are necessary organizational activities, and that today's professionally trained accountants are adequately qualified to fulfil them, it is the broader role as the financial function contained in the Type F approach which deserves analysis. If accountants are not able by education, training and experience to fulfil a role as part of the management team, they will be excluded from organizational decision making, and demand for them from at least the larger industrial and commercial enterprises will be only as relatively narrow, technical experts.

For, in Type F finance departments, accounting tends to be regarded as a specialist, technical activity which, although highly valued, is strictly limited in its organizational role. The primary focus of the wider financial function is, rather, its role in actively promoting earnings and growth. This is achieved through its contribution to the following:

•   financial and strategic planning;

•   new business ideas and developments;

- negotiation of deals arising from planning and new developments;

- treasury and tax management.

One symptom of the changes underway is the structure, organization and orientation of the finance function itself. Increasingly, British companies have adopted the American approach of a division between the accounting, controllership and treasury functions. The last two have less and less to do with accounting *per se*. Management information systems are placing more emphasis on both nonfinancial factors and the need to relate more actively to questions arising from strategic planning and direction. The interface with information processing technology is also becoming more important. Equally, the treasury function is coming to be seen as being of strategic financial importance to the organization rather than a mere tactical means of squeezing out marginal interest rate benefits or shaving fractions of a percent from tax bills.

Aptitudes and Approaches

It is now being recognized that a fully developed finance function needs to contribute towards organization strategy and to act as a profit centre within the organization. Table 6.1 sets out one financial director's perception of the aptitudes and approaches which people in such a finance function need to adopt, and contrasts them with his view of the attitudes and approaches which an accountant's training tends to produce.

Those financial executives who are aware need to ground their perceptions of the world in a broad view of business reality rather than seeing it through the distorting mirror of accounting convention. Because they are future-directed in their thinking, they are always dealing with uncertainties. They tend to think in round numbers and 'ballpark figures' rather than fostering an illusion of spurious accuracy. Consequently, thinking should be directed first towards qualitative analysis of problems, with quantification occurring only when qualitatively acceptable plans have been derived. And where quantification takes place, it should emphasize physical measures — volume, growth, cashflows, and so on — rather than financial results of alternative actions. In all, the good Type F financial executive is a measured risk-taker, indeed one who may well make his or her approach to risk explicit, and he or she is proactive, causing new developments rather than adopting a risk averse attitude to the world and reacting to developments.

Table 6.1 Aptitudes and attitudes contrasted

Type F (finance)	Type A (accounting)
Business reality	Accounting convention
'Ball park' figures	Illusion of accuracy
Numbers last	Numbers first
Physical measures	Financial results
Measured risktaking	Risk avoiding
Proactive	Reactive

To what extent does an accountancy training encourage Type F attitudes rather than Type A attitudes? A few moments' reflection upon the mode of training and the syllabus which accountancy students go through and the work experience they enjoy, perhaps especially the experience of auditing large companies, suggests that the Type F approach is not being encouraged. Accounting examinations are based upon well-defined problems and very largely the answers required are quantitative in nature and require the use of highly specific techniques for their solution. Training for these examinations emphasizes the question-spotting, technique-oriented approach and the fostering of reflection, creativity and other educational virtues tends to be lost in the pressure to maximize the chances of passing the examination. Moreover, the formal body of knowledge underlying professional training is narrow compared with that used by a modern Type F financial executive. Although the attention given to modern financial economics, decision analysis, organizational design and control, and corporate strategy has grown, such areas are still overwhelmed by accounting technique.

Similarly, because much of modern auditing is highly systematized and, as part of quality control, large firms of accountants demand adherence to standard procedures in the auditing of big companies, many student accountants find there is little scope for the development of personal judgement and innovation in the work that they do during their training period.

Many leading practitioners would be at pains to deny the foregoing analysis. They would point to the dangers of planning without the discipline of detailed calculations firmly grounded on existing experience, to the virtues of well-designed financial reporting systems as indicators of actual performance, and to the pitfalls which sometimes occur when businesses over-emphasize physical measurements of performance. Against the charge that accountants do not perceive business reality, many practitioners would counter that accountancy practices are themselves successful entrepreneurial organizations and emphasize the key part which analytical review plays in auditing. A well-conducted analytical review of a business is held to require a very firm grasp of the essentials of the business and the underlying environment in which it must operate. In addition, the success of many accountancy practices in expanding their management consultancy services quite remarkably, demonstrates that there is a real demand from industry for financial and other advisory functions from accountants although, it should be added, some of the large consultancy practices have an equivocal view of the value of the audit trainees of their own firms!

Conclusion

Whatever the merits, or otherwise, of a professional accountancy training from industry's point of view, the growth of a financial management cadre which owes no allegiance to accountancy as its parent discipline is a fact and provides an interesting touch-stone for analysing a number of problems facing the profession.

If industry and commerce cease to demand great numbers of newly and recently qualified accountants, then the numbers of accountants leaving the profession will decrease. This would have very significant consequences for the organization of professional firms which would become top-heavy with qualified accountants having little prospect of career advancement within the profession. In turn, fewer students would be recruited and it is likely that a much higher proportion of the business-minded output of university graduates would enter directly into industry in a financial management stream, thus reinforcing the growth of a separate industrial based financial profession.

In such a situation the work of audit firms would become even more divorced from the day-to-day operations of industry, and the perceptions of firms might alter from that of general financial experts towards that of specialist audit companies. Increasingly within industry the function of the chief accountant would become marginalized and, even as controller of the financial part of the company's management information system, would be vulnerable to attack. Whether or not such developments would lead to better decision making from an overall economic point of view, the ramifications are certainly profound for the accountancy profession.

Of course, the probability of such a drastic set of changes might not be high, if only because the accountancy profession has few competitors. With the present number and size of business schools and the relatively few companies engaged in the serious training of financial executives, most small and medium-sized industrial and commercial enterprises will have to rely on the profession for their financial managers for a long while to come. But the situation in a significant number of large companies is more volatile and the time is now ripe for the profession to ponder on the implications of a large number, if not a majority, of the most senior financial executives in the country being independent of it. At the very least this could have implications for the image of the profession, its attractiveness in the eyes of graduates and, not least, the formulation and policing of accounting policy.

7

The Future of Information Technology and the Accountant

Unless the accountant is content to be pushed aside, to be dispensed with, it behooves him earnestly to grapple with the problem of the application of machinery to office conditions as rapidly as possible to make good use of his opportunities, the wasted opportunities of the past.

L.Dicksee, 1929.

As the quotation shows, concern about the impact of information-processing technology on the accountant is not new. Viewed in an historical context, the sceptic might be forgiven for believing that information technology (IT) was only a further manifestation of a process of the development of information handling which began with the invention of the filing cabinet and the typewriter in the latter part of the nineteenth century. From this perspective, it is important to realize that the improvement of communication and information-handling ability has been a necessary precondition for the evolution of management which has occurred over the last century.

Centralizing Management

No longer are organizations run by quasi-independent managers who are forced to make their own decisions because time and information processing resources do not permit central control. Instead, ever-more sophisticated communication and control structures have increased the potential for central management to control the organization, for good or ill. This is not to say that developments in information processing cannot have a decentralizing tendency, particularly where information becomes communicable to a wider range of people than was previously possible. However, within organizations, where generally no 'Freedom of Information Act' applies, the centralizing tendency seems to be one which predominates, unless some conscious policy of decentralisation is adopted. Whichever tendency is the stronger in a particular situation will depend on a variety of factors, including those referred to in previous chapters, but it is clear that the effects of changes in information handling on decision taking within organizations are profound.

Within the United Kingdom, the accountancy profession has attained a pre-eminent position in the control and checking of organizational information flows. But it is clear that this position is not one which is enjoyed as of right; there are competing occupational groups which may come to have larger and perhaps even dominant positions as information managers if the profession ceases to be as adaptive to developments as it has been in the past.

Because the pace of change arising from the growth of IT is very rapid, the question of adaptation is a particularly urgent one for the profession at present. The implications extend not only to the internal management of organizations but also to the external world, as users of published accounting information begin to rely on databases of company information held on computer rather than full hard-copy reports; pressures for improving the comparability of reports may be expected to increase; and even standard-setters may soon need to come to terms with the IT revolution.

Information Technology

While information technology is the subject of various exhaustive definitions, we can characterize it as the application of computers to the handling of information. Examples include: the batch processing of transactions by mainframe computers, which is, or certainly ought to be, well-understood by accountants; spreadsheets and financial modelling; expert systems; other decision-support systems; computer-aided design/computer-aided manufacturing (CAD/CAM); electronic mail; wordprocessing; databases; and a host of other applications. Most accountants in industry and practice have at least some experience as users of some elements of IT. Indeed, for some users the ubiquitous spreadsheet can proliferate to the point where applications need to be stamped out rather than encouraged. Yet the potential for integrating these applications into a synergistic whole which is greater, or at least different in quality, than its component parts is fundamental to the problems which will face the profession.

The Alvey Programme

The enabling technologies for the enhancement and integration of these applications have been the subject of a government initiative — the Alvey programme — which, by UK standards, has invested large sums in five areas:

1. *Software engineering* — aimed at reducing the cost and improving the quality of new software.

2. *Expert systems* — so called intelligent knowledge-based systems (IKBS), which incorporate the knowledge and decision rules of experts in particular domains of expertise.

3. *Man—machine interface (MMI)* — making computers easier to use and avoiding the need for skilled operators.

4. *Very large-scale integration (VLSI)* — making bigger and much more powerful chips.

5. *Advanced network research* — improving the sharing of information and hardware facilities.

Information Technology is the effect of advances into the 'fifth generation of computing' on these five fronts which the profession now faces. In these developments software is at least as important as hardware. Indeed, it is the development of software which now seems to be the main constraint on the further application of IT in business.

Software development has changed rapidly in character over the past three decades. In the 1950s, the main task of the programmer was to overcome the unreliability of the hardware. With increasing power and reliability of the hardware came the introduction of sophisticated operating systems which stand between the programme and the machine.

In the beginning, operating systems were expensive and unreliable. They also used a great deal of the resources of the machine so that programmers spent much of their time struggling to achieve their objectives within the constraints of the operating system. The problems which the growth of operating systems provided were probably as responsible as poor estimating and control for the reputation for costliness and unreliability which software, as a whole, gained in the mid-1960s, and which it has never truly shaken off.

Since 1975 there has been something of a 'counter-revolution'. For example, the prevalence of the very simple language, Basic; the development of new generations of operating systems such as Unix; and the advent of the personal computer have simplified the task of programming many applications, to the extent of allowing users some opportunity for programme development, even if the relatively unsupported, one-to-one contact with the computer environment is more like that of early machines than the environments which large mainframe applications provide.

At present, software developers are reducing the impact of several limiting factors, and as a result the depth and range of IT applications adopted in organizations will increase.

Achieving accuracy in software is immensely costly. The programmer is faced with a task of writing software which does what the user wants and then of determining whether the instructions he or she has written are correct in achieving the expected result in the wide and unforeseeable combination of circumstances which the user will encounter. Software writing is a technology where, hitherto, scientific proof has not been available as a means of verifying the correctness of what has been done. Yet there is hope that forms of proof of the logical correctness of software will emerge which will be capable of being applied to commercial-sized programmes.

Improvement in programming productivity is the subject of immense effort through the development of high-level languages beyond the familiar Fortran and Cobol and the development of programmers' 'workbenches' in the form of improved hardware and software combinations to take care of the necessary housekeeping in programming.

More Power Please

Despite enormous improvements in hardware capabilities there is still a need to obtain more power from software. Each time machine performance improves, software is rapidly developed to take advantage of the improvement and machine limitations currently prevent the development of many interesting applications. For example, moving colour graphics are immensely demanding of machine memory and processing, and for artificial intelligence applications the development of machine architectures to obey new software structures are underway. Consequently software designers are always striving to improve performance within existing architectures, which, like that of IBM, may have been defined up to twenty-five years ago.

Software maintenance, an unglamorous topic, is a real limitation to progress. Maintenance is not just keeping software in its original condition but involves the ability to add to and change the capabilities of software. Badly developed software, where only dim traces of the structure of the programme can be found, may be very costly to modify with any assurance of continued reliability of working. To this extent the brilliant can be the enemy of the good. There is a constant need to tame genius with the discipline of good husbandry. A viable programmer's workbench will incorporate tools to store a model of programme structure.

Transferring software from one type of machine to another is a perennial problem. Here great progress has been made, for example, by the development of programmes in the Unix environment — which is a keystone of the strategy for survival of non-IBM members of the industry.

Software packages are the most important response to the limitations just described. Although they may demand that the user, to a certain extent, tailors the problem to the package rather than the other way round, the availability of standards solutions greatly reduces the cost of software to the user.

The Impact on the Accountant in Industry

It is already possible to discern changes that IT has made on the role of the accountant in industry, and these trends may be expected to continue. Initially, computers were introduced into industry to record transactions. Their use has evolved to include some aspects of the planning of future strategy and tactics and now extends to the actual carrying out of transactions.

As IT becomes still more integrated into the actual processes of business, so transactions records will become the by-product of production and exchange operations. For the accountant there is a potential for improved control, since the recording of events becomes a necessary consequence of their occurrence; but flexibility may be lost if information production becomes dependent upon operational constraints and a much more informed understanding of the organizational aspects of information processing will be required.

The growth of the software package as a cost-reducing solution to data processing needs has already caused reductions in the number of systems development staff in some organizations. Again, control is improved but flexibility is lost since the user of a package may, in general, not be able to alter it; errors and fraud cannot be introduced, but also the package cannot be tailored to individual needs to the same extent as a custom-designed system.

The growth of communications offers the potential for both a simplification and extension of some treasury operations. In an information-intensive financial environment the treasury function might become an even more strategic one. At the same time companies may find it possible to automate or subcontract some of their treasury operations to financial institutions.

In the longer term, expert systems developments and a growing ability to interrogate external databases will offer people within organizations access to a much wider range of expertise and information than it is presently feasible to maintain in-house. While other business disciplines (production, marketing, personnel, etc.) will benefit from the wider availability of more knowledge and expertise, the accountant is probably particularly well-placed to develop and use the potentialities of these new sources for the benefit of his or her organization.

The implications of the rampant growth of networks and the consequent dispersion of organizations in physical and group allegiance terms are that people in organizations will develop new ways of working. This change and the need which will follow to impose new forms of organizational control will involve the accountant as much as anyone within the business.

The Impact on the Accountant in the Profession

As users of information technology, accountants in the profession will be subject to the same forces as accountants in industry. Internal systems will change; office automation may increase productivity (although the evidence is equivocal). Training will benefit from developments in computer-assisted learning. The range, depth and updating of publications will improve as costs of small-scale publication activities decrease.

In their businesses, however, accountants will face a number of challenges. Competition will increase. We have already seen attempts by financial institutions to offer transactions processing and financial advice in competition with accountants. Although the effects on the business of firms are still emerging, the move is symptomatic of a tendency for businesses in the financial services sector, including accountants, to increase the diversity of the services they offer. Information Technology is one of the enabling technologies for increased competition because it reduces the economies of scale which have been effective barriers to entry into particular fields. For professional accountants this is as much an opportunity as a threat since it enables them to offer advisory services in areas which have been traditionally the preserve of, for example, merchant banks.

Firms are also able to undertake more of their own software development. In particular, savings may be made if knowledge can be embodied in expert systems or other decision-support software, which will enable firms to increase the productivity and reliability of their staff — a factor of some importance in the present employment and legal environment. In addition, such developments might also result in saleable products. Indeed, some firms are already beginning to publish their own decision-support software.

Large firms' core business of auditing will, of course, be affected as much as the other activities of firms. Most firms have come to grips with the problems of auditing mainframe systems, but as yet microcomputers still present control and security problems. Increased regulation is in prospect both through legislation and through professional standards. New regulations will control not only the way in which auditing is done, but new controls on clients may extend the role of the auditor in monitoring client behaviour on behalf of third parties.

However, there is the possibility that aspects of the audit can be automated, for example, the checking from trial balance to final accounts, and this will have implications for the staffing and organization of firms. Firms will begin to need fewer but more highly trained staff. At present there is a need for intelligent but not necessarily very skilled staff on some audit work — this need will decrease. On the other hand, there will be a need for decision-support in audit planning and the need for particular skills will increase the pressure for specialization. Communications developments will bring enhanced audit opportunities as it becomes possible to interrogate clients' computer systems from the auditor's office.

The Institute's Role

It is doubtful whether the Institute could or should attempt to exercise much influence on the development of IT applications or their commercial exploitation. However, the Institute needs to react to the needs of its members in relation to education, organization and publicity.

Information Technology is one of a number of topics for which a 'front loaded' educational pattern would be appropriate. The initial skill-level required of chartered students is increasing and firms are finding it more difficult to provide the training ground for the acquisition of skills. A period of full-time training prior to work experience would provide the opportunity for the incorporation of a distinct paper in the syllabus on the use of technology in business and the opportunity for hands-on training.

The current considerations of the organization of the Institute will also need to recognize IT as one of the factors providing pressure for the acceptance of specialization, if only to emphasize the role of accountants in IT applications development. A continuing publicity effort will be required to remind the business community and accountants themselves of that role.

8

The Future of Accounting Standards

The accounting standard-setting movement has recently passed through turbulent times and many people are now beginning to wonder if private sector standard-setting has lost its way. In the last ten years the Accounting Standards Committee (ASC) and, more generally, the professional bodies have instigated a number of reviews of the process of setting, standards, the most recent of which is found in the Dearing Report (ICAEW, 1988)[1]. In this chapter the present state of standard-setting is analysed with a view to considering its likely future development.

The development of standard-setting has followed a roughly similar course in Britain and in the United States. In the late 1960s and early 1970s in both nations, bodies which made relatively weak recommendations on external financial reporting were replaced by more authoritative accounting standard-setting bodies. In both cases, initial standards were set which dealt with pressing problems of financial measurement and disclosure. The solutions were devised without being founded on a theoretical framework which specified the objectives of financial reporting or the contribution which accounting standards were supposed to make to those objectives, or even any sustained body of research and inquiry. This approach has often been described as 'putting out bushfires'. The American

1   This chapter was written prior to the publication of the review of standard-setting chaired by Sir Ron Dearing. The main issues discussed in the chapter are still relevant tot he future of accounting standards, although that review obviously influences the context in which they must be resolved.

Financial Accounting Standards Board (FASB) has subsequently attempted to provide quite explicitly some agreed objectives for financial reporting, while the more cautious British body has made an occasional more implicit nod in that direction. Indeed, the FASB has gone on to attempt to construct a 'conceptual framework' for financial reporting in the hope that such an agreed framework would make standard-setting easier and standards more logically consistent.

Despite the considerable publicity and controversy that has surrounded their activities at times, both the FASB and the ASC can claim some successes in providing standards which temporarily, at least, narrow down the diversity of accounting practice and disclosure. However, there have been notable failures, most outstandingly in failing to arrive at an agreed system of accounting for changing prices but also in other areas. In the United States standards have, in effect, been legally enforced on public companies through the requirements of the Securities and Exchange Commission, but there has been no compulsion for private companies to follow standards. In the United Kingdom what enforcement there has been has occurred through attempts at self-regulation by the accounting community and perhaps, as a result, has been much less rigorous so far as public companies are concerned.

There has been a growing concern by some observers that UK standard-setting is dominated by the views of preparers of accounts — companies and auditors — and that the views of users — investors, investment analysts and others — are being increasingly unheard. At the same time it is perceived that the spirit, and often the letter, of standards is being flouted by a growing minority of companies through the use of ingenious loopholes in standards or by outright non-compliance. Indeed, creative accounting is now something that is quite openly talked about in the private sector, in the public sector, and in relation to those preprivatization accounts that helped to provide a conduit between the two. It is as if a new confidence allows a wider public awareness of what was hushed up until recently — that accounting has the potential to be a moveable device at the service of particular interests.

The ASC had its beginnings in accounting controversy and one of its achievements was to deflect criticism away from the profession. There is now a danger that increasing non-compliance with standards, and not least the increasingly public manner in which this is being done and its increasing association in the public eye with the marketing and competitive strategies of the accounting firms that the Wall Street *Journal* now calls the 'audit business', will again call into question the ability of the profession to regulate itself.

The future development of standard-setting will depend on the views of members of the profession and users of accounts on a number of key questions which are to be outlined below. It will also depend on the degree of consensus which exists on those questions and other potentially controversial matters. Where consensus exists, it may be possible to mobilize action on that basis such that standard-setting might continue to be viewed as a worthy and worthwhile activity with a moderately high claim to attention and resources. If there is little agreement on fundamental matters, then standard-setting may provide accounting with an unpleasantly high public profile or the standards movement may wither away.

In the rest of this review we concentrate on accounting standards for quoted companies; the problem of what small companies should report is another question. However, if standards become more detailed and more onerous to comply with, it seems unlikely that in the long term small companies could be expected to suffer the full rigours of financial reporting.

What are Financial Statements for?

A feature of the standards movement has been a loose agreement that the purpose of financial statements is to provide users of accounts with information to assist them in making decisions. While some lip service has been paid to the needs of other classes of decision makers, the predominant user groups with a claim on the concerns of standard-setters have been investors, potential investors and their advisors. This decision-usefulness view of financial statements is of relatively recent origin — or at least its appeal to and use by practitioners is. Prior to 1970 it is probable that the received wisdom as to the purpose of accounts was that they showed the quality of the stewardship of the company's assets exercised by the directors. Indeed, the ASC was itself born amid the traumas created by the shift from one way of viewing accounting to the other. In the context of business mergers and the economic interventionist policies of the state, people started to appeal to accounting as a form of economic intelligence — only to realize the limits on the intelligence that shaped its form.

Now there are even some indications that the decision-usefulness view is on the wane. A growing understanding of the pricing mechanism in the stock market casts doubt on the value of financial statements for making investment decisions. By and large most investment analysts and professional investors now recognize that the stock market is reasonably efficient at pricing securities based on available information, at least in terms of a restrictive meaning of efficiency. And there is a lot more information available about companies than their annual reports and accounts. One of the reasons that the voice of users has not been heard loudly is that members of the professional investing community do not care very deeply about the minutiae of published financial statements because they have access to copious alternative sources of information. Another reason is that there are contradictions in reconciling the objective of obtaining information for future-directed decisions with the current kind of financial statements, as the progress of the FASB's conceptual framework has shown.

At the same time it is becoming recognized that accounting choices can affect the well-offness of different groups whether they are users of the accounts or not. In such cases the imposition of accounting standards can have what economists call 'welfare effects'. The legitimacy of a private sector, self-regulating group making these choices for society is clearly open to question and weakens the hand of the ASC in attempting to impose standards. For example, the debate on inflation accounting has at various times involved different interest groups seeking to support or oppose general indexation, to demonstrate the anorexia of British manufacturing industry, to obtain favourable tax changes or conceal the effects of inflation on borrowings. Setting standards is much more than a disinterested seeking after improved methods of profit measurement.

Finally, something of a return to a stewardship view of accounting is beginning. The importance of the role of accounting in facilitating contracts which do not take place in markets as efficient as the stock market is becoming more widely appreciated. Such markets include the market for loan capital and the takeover market. Companies' negotiations with regulatory agencies can also be regarded as a market for this purpose. The independent monitoring of the outcome of events makes it possible to enter into agreements which could not otherwise exist.

Disagreement about the fundamental purpose of financial statements and accounting standards will be one factor which will tend to reduce consensus about the whole of the standard-setting area.

What Kinds of Financial Statements?

Many people lay great emphasis on the way in which UK accounting is based on the undefined concept of the 'true and fair view'. We manage by and large with rather few rules which tend to be of the nature of broad principles rather than detailed sets of rules. This approach is in contrast to the systems of continental Europe which are heavily reliant on rules. Even though the EC Fourth Directive includes the so-called 'true and fair override', the conception that accounts could comply with measurement and disclosure rules yet not show a true and fair view is incomprehensible to the large body of continental accountants.

The American system of accounting, although Anglo-Saxon in origin, is also much more reliant on rules than is the British system. The American 'fair presentation in accordance with generally accepted accounting principles' refers to a more detailed body of rules than the United Kingdom's 'true and fair view'. Nevertheless, although the Americans would appear to have less need than the British for codification and generalization of principles, it is they who have made most progress in creating a 'conceptual framework' for financial reporting. Such a framework, if successful, would provide, in the eyes of some, the broad principles from which accounting standards and resulting accounting practice could be deduced in a coherent and consistent manner. In the United Kingdom, while the ASC has monitored the progress of the US conceptual framework project, it has shown little formal commitment to promoting equivalent development here, although recently the professional bodies themselves initiated their own investigations of general conceptual approaches to accounting problems (ICAS, 1988; Solomons, 1989).

For the future, the UK system of standards could potentially develop as a rule-based system where it is possible to foresee the promulgation of a multitude of detailed rules specific to particular kinds of transactions and industrial groupings. Alternatively, codification of existing practice may lead to the crystallization of broad principles which become enforced either explicitly or implicitly by law or the accounting community and give rise to relatively uniform accounting practices. On balance, it seems most likely that rules will expand in number and detail. Both the climate of regulation in the City and growing pressure for internationalization and harmonization point to an increase in regulation. In the past in the United Kingdom, control of enterprises has been debated in terms of ownership. That era may now be over; control is now much more a question of regulation, as in the United States.

Growth in regulation would tend to make the 'true and fair' conception appear increasingly anachronistic. There is not so much room for respect of judgement in a regulated environment. It is in any event becoming increasingly difficult to defend the idea that a company has made a certain sum of profit for a financial year which can be ascertained and portrayed truly by accountants independently of measurement rules.

Failure to develop in one or other of the above directions would merely lead to a growing diversity of practice, financial reporting anarchy, collapse of credibility in the system and its eventual replacement by some other system of control.

How will Standards be Enforced?

The question of the kind of standards that will be imposed leads naturally to the question of how rigorously standards will be enforced. In the current climate, enforcement is mainly of the 'club membership' variety. The penalties which transgressors from the letter of standards face are seldom severe. The apparent enforcers of standards, the auditors, have only a bludgeon to wield, namely audit qualification. And even that, when finally brought to bear, turns out to be made of foam rubber as often as not. Transgression of the spirit of standards, which is the foundation of the British and Irish 'broad principles' system, turns out to be even more weakly penalized. Few auditors seem willing to push to the limits of qualification of the financial statements an opinion that a treatment which complies with the letter of a standard does not show a true and fair view. Diversity of opinion among even the largest firms about allowable alternative treatments makes the broad principles view appear even less effective.

In consequence it seems that the only possibility, apart from continuation of the existing trend away from compliance with standards, is some improvement in enforcement and that any set of scenarios involving standards must include more rigid enforcement as a likely development.

The question of the degree of enforcement is logically distinct from that of 'who will do the enforcing?' In a more rigorous enforcement climate, the state, either directly or through an intermediate agency, is an obvious candidate, but it is possible that another body could achieve greater compliance if there were sufficient incentive for the preparing and auditing community to accede to such an authority. There are a number of possible means by which this could be achieved. More effort could be expended in achieving consensus, although this would certainly lead to a more drawn out standard-setting process and more influence being exercised by powerful interest groups. More 'due process' in the form of detailed consultation and public hearings could be implemented, but such a route tends to end in legal wrangling. A successful conceptual framework could persuade preparers of the 'ineluctable logic', to quote a previous chairman of the ASC, of standards set, but the example of FASB's attempt is not propitious. However, it is difficult to see what incentive could ensure success for such moves except the threat of state intervention. The problems of legitimacy, such as the ASC has at present, would remain.

Who will set Standards?

There is a growing view that the current divided responsibility for setting financial reporting requirements is illogical and untenable. Company law now lays down a few principles and a very large number of detailed rules about the content of company financial statements. It leaves to the Accounting Standards Committee some very important matters, for example inflation accounting and accounting for acquisition and mergers, so far with disappointing results. 'Poisoned chalices' will continue to be passed back and forth between the DTI and the ASC so long as a division of responsibilities exists.

As the view increases that the profession has no mandate to set standards for people who are not members of it, so failures of enforcement will increase and with them pressure for more state involvement in both setting and enforcement. While standard-setting was viewed purely as a technical matter such views could be resisted, but they may not be for much longer. The profession's lack of authority for social regulation and potentially wealth redistributing decisions has already become evident over such matters as whether the ASC has the competence to proscribe accounting treatments permitted in the Companies Act and in pressures for wider representation of interest groups on the ASC.

Recent developments in the regulation of the City and financial services also lend credence to the view that independent self-regulated standard-setting may become outmoded. Deficiencies in standards or their enforcement will draw attention to the standard-setting process and increase the attention which is paid to standards by, for example, the Securities and Investments Board.

Growing internationalization, one of the key factors which has been identified as shaping the economic future, also implies a reduction in the autonomy of the ASC. International trade and investment will increasingly require internationally acceptable and understandable financial statements. Standards will either need to provide for more harmonization than at present or, increasingly, one nation's system will come to predominate. That nation will be the United States.

Conclusion

Who would have predicted in 1965 that controversies about accounting principles would have led to the setting up of the ASC in 1969? By the same token, it is by no means certain that accounting standards will seem important in the year 2000. Conflicts of economic interest which gave rise to the accounting standards movement may move to other arenas. It is possible, for example, that the roles of auditors or non-executive directors will become controversial while standard-setting languishes in a comparative backwater of concern.

Alternatively, there may be a period of turbulence from which it becomes clear that the current system of standard-setting cannot emerge intact. Individual standards and the standard-setting process could become controversial. The enforcement and/or the setting of standards could come under state influence to a much greater degree that at present. Events which could trigger such a change include increasing pressure for internationalization, a series of major financial scandals or a major failure to react to changing accounting needs, for example caused by a resurgence of inflation or increasingly sophisticated off-balance sheet financing arrangements. On balance it seems unlikely that the current regime of standard-setting and enforcement will continue substantially unchanged in the long term.

References

Institute of Chartered Accountants in England and Wales (ICAEW) (1988), *The Making of Accounting Standards*, Report of the Review Committee under the Chairmanship of Sir Ron Dearing.

Institute of Chartered Accountants of Scotland (ICAS) (1988), *Making Corporate Reports Valuable*, Kogan Page.

Solomons, D. (1989), *Guidelines for Decisions in Financial Reporting*, ICAEW Research Board.

9

The Future of Accounting
and the City

There are likely to be few readers of this chapter who are not aware of the radical changes which have occurred and are occurring in the financial services industry. The general nature of the changes is well-known: the technology for dealing in the stock market and the commission system for securities traders changed in the so-called 'Big Bang', the securities markets are becoming ever more international, and the Financial Services Act has introduced a new era of regulation. However, the detail of these changes and the implications which they are likely to have are not so well known. So rapid are these changes that this chapter is likely to be out of date before it appears in print.

The Role of the City

The financial services industry has grown rapidly over the recent past, both in absolute terms and as a proportion of Britain's gross national product. The City is at once a source of funds for industry, a means whereby savers can invest funds and yet retain a degree of liquidity, and a source of foreign earnings by provision of these services internationally.

Because of its size the City is clearly a powerful force for good or ill and in Chapter 3 we noted the key role which it would play in determining Britain's economic future. To maintain its present importance the City must not only remain competitive in the services which it provides. It must also maintain the public perception of respectability and legitimacy which pervades its work.

Recent scandals relating to insider dealing and behaviour during takeovers have crystallized concern as to whether financial markets can be relied upon to regulate themselves. Control of the fairness and propriety with which markets operate is widely seen as a necessary condition for the City to maintain its place as the third leg of the three-legged stool of world markets comprising New York, Tokyo and London which permits global twenty-four-hour trading.

The Impact on Accounting

The relationship between the City and the accounting profession is important for both groups. In times past, the functions of the groups were separate but, increasingly, accounting firms have come to provide services and advice which were formerly the province of merchant banks. Moreover, the growth of in-house treasury operations in large companies, frequently but not always staffed by accountants, has led to some financial functions being provided in-house rather than in the City.

Nevertheless the traditional functions which the profession performs for the City remain, that is to say as independent providers of financial information and as part of the City's own regulatory process.

The forces for change which are having and will have the most impact on accounting are: the regulation of the financial services industry (including the accounting profession), 'globalization', and technological change.

Regulation of Financial Services

The most immediate force for change in a large section of the profession is the regime of regulation which came into being as a result of the Financial Services Act 1986. Compliance with the Act is a new factor shaping the future of accounting. It affects firms in those aspects of their operations which are designated as investment business under the Act and in their role as advisors and auditors of clients carrying on investment business.

The Act's definition of investment business is a very wide one and most firms which offer investment advice to their clients have found that they need to be authorized to carry on that business.

Three alternative routes to authorization were available: direct authorization by the Securities and Investments Board (SIB), membership of a self-regulatory organization (SRO), or membership of a recognized professional body (RPB). In practice direct authorization is impracticable for the majority of firms, if not all firms, and while it is possible that some larger firms with diverse activities may be attracted by joining a SRO most firms will want to be authorized by virtue of their affiliation to the Institute, which has therefore become a RPB.

This action has had implications for all Institute members, since as a consequence the Institute's disciplinary rules, code of ethics and training and admission requirements must be at least as rigorous as those for direct authorization. Similar requirements apply to the other accountancy bodies, so the Act has given a powerful impetus for convergence. The duplication of compliance costs in different bodies was an important influence on the initiation of merger discussions between the English and Scottish Institutes. Even if attempts were made to confine the additional rules to those members who wished to be recognized as falling within their province, experience suggests that it would be difficult to maintain such a distinction over any length of time.

Not least of the Act's effects is that upon the balance between external regulation and self-regulation. Although the Act is at considerable pains to preserve the appearance of a self-regulated system, the SIB is in practice extremely powerful. Notwithstanding its form as a company limited by guarantee, the SIB is likely to develop much as an arm of the state and the ability of the City and professions to set and enforce their own standards will diminish considerably.

Professional firms will take part in the process of regulation as auditors and accountants. The Act empowers auditors to inform the relevant regulatory authority of any matters which are relevant to its function in relation to individual clients. This represents a fundamental change in the auditor—client relationship, since the auditor is no longer acting purely for a client and its shareholders, but will be a watchdog on behalf of an external party. Such a change is not going to be easy for many members of the profession to digest.

As far as SIB is concerned, the precise form, meaning and implications of some of the new audit requirements are still subject to considerable discussion. Indeed, these are likely to be incorporated in the first instance into the rules of the professional bodies (see, for example, the draft auditing guideline 'The implications for auditors of the Financial Services Act, 1986', *Accountancy*, February 1988). But as is happening with similar rules applicable to building societies and banks, the audit function is going to extend beyond the provision of a simple opinion on the financial statements. As well as reporting on the handling of client money and continuous compliance with minimum capital requirements the auditor seems bound, eventually, to acquire a responsibility for detecting and reporting to supervisory authorities fraud and failures of internal control and other management controls. The cloaks of materiality and disclosure may cease to be available once there is a breach of the 'Maginot line' defence that the auditor's duty is solely to form an opinion on the accounts. It scarcely needs pointing out that the nature of the client—auditor relationship cannot be but profoundly affected by this change. Auditors will be forced to adopt much more rigorous standards of independence from clients.

Access of auditors to regulators raises obvious issues. In practice in what circumstances will the auditor go to the regulator without telling the client? Will the client accompany the auditor when he or she talks to the regulator? What access will regulators have to the papers (e.g. internal audit and compliance reports) of investment businesses and of their auditors?

The change of relationship between auditor and client could well be a painful one. The City is itself being forced to adapt its ways in line with modern standards. Investment businesses, with the help of consultants, will need to continue to develop new internal systems to monitor and control compliance with new business standards in a more competitive environment.

The Big Bang occurred during the strongest Bull market since the 1920s; the post-'Big Bang' City is now experiencing the trauma of adjusting to a very different market situation. The events of 'Black Monday' changed many peoples' experience of the City and have had continuing effects on employment. With a large number of players in a market where there are thinner margins, the new market context might itself provide temptations for those inclined to cut corners. As things stand, accountants might well be perceived as forming an important line of defence against cheating, with the consequence that many accountants — both in the role of auditors and in the compliance function of investment businesses — will be faced with difficult ethical and business problems. Although the Financial Services Act has ensured that investment businesses will need more audit services, they will be of a different kind from existing audits. People and firms will need considerable support if they are not to bend the rules in favour of the short term economic interests of their organizations or their clients.

Any well-publicized failures of the system of regulation could have severe effects on the extent to which the City continues to be seen as a productive sector of the economy, and in such a situation the role of accountants might acquire an uncomfortably high profile.

It seems unlikely that the presentation of accounts by listed and other publicly traded companies will be unaffected by SIB. It is not yet the case that SIB will require adherence to accounting standards by all listed companies, which would thus effectively give standards legal force for those companies. However, it is more than likely that all businesses required to register will be subject to compliance with standards, if only through a more explicit conception of the meaning of the true and fair requirement. Extension of such a requirement to all traded companies may be difficult to resist, particularly if accounting procedures by such companies continue to be controversial. For example, failure by the ASC to achieve consensus among accountants and lawyers about off-balance sheet finance could well be viewed by SIB as an issue which required it to step in, thus precipitating explicit SIB involvement in standard-setting. It may be assumed that the regulators will have an immediate implicit influence on standards.

Globalization and Technological Change

The globalisation of financial markets is not of itself new. The process has been proceeding for more than twenty years since the development of the Euro-currency market in the 1960s. What is new is the impact of technological change which has increased the speed and volume of transactions immensely. The development of twenty-four-hour markets based on London, Tokyo and New York has resulted in an enormous expansion of the representation of financial houses internationally.

So far as accountants are concerned it is useful to distinguish between the developments in the secondary and primary (new issue) markets. In the secondary market, technology means that markets are more difficult to control in one sense because the volume of transactions and the physical dispersion of traders make it difficult to know what is going on in real time. On the other hand fuller recording of transactions and the development of software to analyse patterns of trading will mean that in future it will be easier to trace the history of deals and market operations. International sharing of quotations is already beginning, and continued technological progress is inevitable. As already noted, one of its effects will be to increase competition in the market-place and, inevitably, this will increase the tension between the 'entrepreneurial' and the 'prudential' for financial institutions. It must be the goal of regulators to insure that the 'prudential' is not outweighed by the seeking of profit. Agreements between the DTI and the SEC for the sharing of information must be welcomed as a beginning of international cooperation in the regulation of markets. The development of international clearing arrangements for transactions will make such international cooperation especially important.

For the longer term, future technological developments in financial reporting seem likely to become significant. The SEC already permits certain filings by electronic means and it is not difficult to see that there will be a move towards more dynamic reporting of information. We can foresee larger firms making voluntary disclosures weekly or more frequently, and users accessing filings through sophisticated data retrieval systems.

Technology also provides additional impetus to a current trend for investment businesses to carry out more functions in-house. While no diminution in the work of professional firms in accounting and other businesses is foreseen, the proportion of 'professional' work done in-house is likely to increase and the professions will find a growing need to cater for members who are staff members of business organizations but who face the ethical and other problems faced by members of professional firms.

Primary markets may concern accountants more. As it becomes more common to seek to issue securities on more than one exchange some common regulation of new issue documents becomes urgent. The SEC has already sought opinion on whether a common prospectus approach or reciprocal acceptance of prospectuses between the United States, Canada and the United Kingdom would be preferable. However, the importance of individual state's jurisdictions in agreeing to any harmonization of prospectus rules will make agreement difficult to achieve, given the differences between generally accepted accounting principles in those countries and the inevitable demand for extension of similar arrangements to other major financial centres.

Because of the domination of the United States and the central role played by accounting principles, auditing standards and auditor independence in the US disclosure system, those factors will need to be addressed in the United Kingdom.

In addition to increased support for international accounting standards, particular concerns about management advisory services carried out by auditors, the need for audit committees, and some form of peer review procedure for audit quality control are all likely to become more topical issues. In this respect the pressures noted in previous chapters towards placing greater emphasis on the need for more independence and control of audit engagements will be reinforced.

Conclusion

The new world which the City faces can be seen as a result of the forces of technology and globalization, which in part is also a result of technological progress. Together these forces have given rise to a new system of financial regulation. There is a formidable current of change in the financial services sector and adaption to new circumstances is likely to require firm guidance if it is not to be painful. Accountants have important roles to play in helping the new system of regulation to operate and in reacting to the other impacts of globalization and technology. The trend towards more regulations at a higher level of detail is probably not one which can be resisted. Despite this there seems bound to be some scandals which will arise. Although the system of control which has been introduced reduces the autonomy of the City and professions, enough remains of the self-regulatory system that it can have a critical effect on the frequency of such scandals, the reaction of regulators to them, and the standing of the City as an international financial centre. In this respect the response of the profession to the changes in the City will be critical to the importance of the role which it can expect to play in international financial services in future.

PART THREE

Overview

10

On Trying to Conceive of Accounting in Motion[1]

Considering the future of accounting is not an easy task. Not only is accounting a changing phenomenon, but also relatively little is known about the forces which put it into motion. Yet in a policy context, such as that for which the Understanding a Changing Environment Group was established, it is just such insights which are needed if the aim is to explore those mobilizing factors which it might be possible to influence and to understand at least some of the implications of those which are not.

While it may often seem comforting to emphasize the certainties of the technical and institutional features of the accounting here and now, that simply does not assist more policy-orientated discussions. That is particularly the case if the intention is to gain some appreciation of the forces by which just such certainties are both created and then questioned, disrupted and changed into new ones. That very process is not only one that has occurred on several occasions in the fairly recent past, but is also one that is a central feature of the accounting present.

Seemingly caught in the midst of both national and international restructurings of economic life, it is hardly surprising that accounting, as a dominant mode of economic calculation in the societies in which we live, should be subject to disruption and change.

1   The discussions of the Understanding a Changing Environment Group provided a stimulating context for reflecting on many of the thoughts and ideas presented in this chapter. We would also like to acknowledge the very helpful comments made on an earlier draft by David Cooper and Mark Dirsmith.

Accounting is entering into new spheres of economic and social life. New roles are being created for both accounting and accountants. Questions are being raised about the appropriateness of the knowledge bases underlying accounting and the educational and developmental processes by which they are instilled and renewed. The institutional structures of the professionalized core of accountancy are subject to both questioning and change. Modes of governance, the domains for professional regulation, the extent of the professional sphere of authority, and the relationships between the profession and the state are now actively on the policy agenda. Competitive forces are also a more visible and salient feature of professional life, raising new dilemmas, putting new pressures on existing institutional forms, and resulting in new elaborations of accounting practices and the bodies of knowledge which are incorporated within them. Moreover, such transformations are, increasingly, not only subject to forces operating within the nation state but also to those stemming from the growing internationalization of business and the financial markets. Key aspects of the accountancy profession can no longer be appreciated in purely national terms. The internationalization of the major audit firms, the increasingly important role played by financial information and controls in the internationalization of business, the global orientation of the financial markets, and the pressures created by supra-national regulation agencies have to be recognized as significant features of the accounting here and now.

Seen in such a context, accounting policy making requires more than an appreciation of the current status quo. It requires an ability to conceive of how things have come to be and how they might become. As is illustrated in Figure 10.1, it requires an informed appreciation of the factors which constrain accounting to be as it is, which put pressures on accounting to become what it was not, and which provide room for discretion and choice within the accountancy profession's own sphere of influence. Rather than emphasizing only what is, a proactive policy orientation requires a more dynamic view of accounting which places the technical and institutional here and now in the context of the forces out of which it emerged and to which it contributes an active enabling force.

Recognizing such arguments, the Institute of Chartered Accountants in England and Wales established the Understanding a Changing Environment Group to provide a platform for the discussion of key features of the accounting context, the changes which were occurring in them, their implications for accounting, and the resultant significant spheres for professional policy formulation and decision making. Although the Group itself had no direct policy role, it was hoped that bringing together senior members of the

profession with influential decision makers from other spheres of life
and experts on particularly important areas of change would provide
a stimulus for professional reflection and policy-orientated thought.

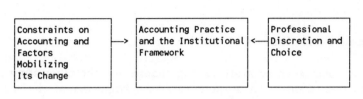

Figure 10.1 The Accounting Context

Some of the results of the discussions of the Group have been
summarized in earlier chapters. The role of this final chapter is to
provide some insight into, and reflection on, the factors which
influenced the choice of activities for the Group and the issues for its
deliberation.

Being aware of the fact that a policy and future-orientated
consideration of professional accountancy is a relatively new
phenomenon, the subsequent discussion comments on some of the
difficulties which such considerations must face, illustrating these by
reflecting on the dilemmas which would have been faced by earlier
members of the profession trying to anticipate some of the key
features of the accounting here and now. Drawing on this illustration
and other understandings of the accounting past, an attempt is made
to identify at least some of the key features implicated in the
processes by which accounting becomes what it was not. Particular
consideration is given to the, often unanticipated, nature of accounting change, the role which both longer term structural trends and
more temporally confined crises have played in disrupting the path
of accounting development, the centrality of the relationship between
accounting and the state, and, not least in significance, the roles
played by the skilful and entrepreneurial nature of accountants. It is
then argued that such insights into past and current accounting
changes, partial though they may still be, nevertheless have a
number of significant implications for the structuring of policy-
orientated discussions of accounting in general and the activities of
the Understanding a Changing Environment Group in particular.
These are briefly reviewed and illustrated in the context of the
Group's activities.

The chapter concludes by recognizing that the factors mobilizing accounting change are themselves not static. Some consideration is therefore given not only to some more recent influences on accounting, but also to the resultant implications which such a turbulent and changing context has for the management of change in the profession.

Some Preliminary Observations

Any consideration of accounting change and the accounting future must be posited on a quite explicit recognition of the fact that accounting is not an isolated technical phenomenon. Consideration must be given to the fact that accounting and its institutional manifestations are deeply embedded in the contexts in which they operate.

The organization of economic and social relationships and the nature of the ties between industry, finance and the state have both influenced and, equally significantly, been influenced in turn by the accounting craft. The degree of contention about economically orientated modes of action, conceptions of governmental economic roles, and the focus of the shifting boundaries between the realms of the public and the private are also factors that have made accounting what it is and, as we are now seeing, will continue to play a significant role in helping it to become what it presently is not. For accounting is one of the most significant forms of economic calculation in society and thus it should not be surprising that it is both reflective of and, at times, influential in the shaping of quite central aspects of economic and social life.

Significant though such wider forces may be for providing a context for accounting change, policy-orientated considerations of accounting must also recognize that the nature of such relationships is unfortunately not well understood at present. That in itself represents quite a major constraint on the possibility of gaining a more proactive view of accounting in motion. Some of the mobilizing forces behind accounting change also receive relatively little public discussion and are even, on occasions, surrounded by an aura of professional mystery. However understandable that may be, it nevertheless does not ease the task of understanding accounting in a more dynamic sense. For attempts to preserve an impression of technical autonomy and neutrality also constrain discussions of the wider factors which so frequently impinge on the accounting here and now.

Our comprehension of accounting is also constrained by the fact that it is a phenomenon that has many roles and consequences.

Although accounting discussions now tend to be graced by appeals to rationale embedded in notions of accountability and the facilitation of economic and financial decision making, these hardly do justice to the full range of wider involvements and functions of such an influential form of economic calculation.

People do not merely perceive that they need accounting in any absolute sense. They argue about it. At times they struggle for particular accounting disclosures. They fight for particular accounting representations of activities, and they are sometimes acutely conscious of the consequences of particular accounts. Yet such a view of accounting is so often masked in discussions of it. The generality of so much of the official accounting discourse has an uneasy relationship to the accounting actuality. Thus any policy-orientated view of accounting ideally needs to be one that can confront the specific as well as the general. It needs to be able to face and address the actuality of the full range of pressures on accounting. That, however, represents quite a challenge at the present time.

Policy-orientated discussions of accounting are also complicated by the fact that accounting is involved in contested decisions which have differential effects. Being implicated in processes of both corporate and social governance, accounting is known to be much more than a merely revelatory endeavour, however little this is discussed. Put simply, people at times argue about the 'realities' which accounting is at least attributed as having the capability to construct rather than merely reveal. Indeed, it is just such an often unmentionable fact that provides one reason for endowing accountants with a certain privileged position and wanting them to engage in modes of operation that create an impression of independence and neutrality.

A Changing Accounting

Such constraints on our understanding of the processes of accounting change are not the only difficulties facing an attempt to gain a more future-orientated view of accounting at the present time. As has already been indicated, accounting and its professional context are themselves changing a great deal, seemingly confronting a turbulence that itself adds appreciably to the difficulty of trying to track possible paths to the future. At the very least, many significant parts of the accounting agenda are in a state of flux.

The nature of a professionalized accountancy is being discussed. Consideration is being given to the governance structures of the professional institutes. The institutional structure of the profession is also being actively deliberated. The boundaries between the regulatory roles of the state, the profession, and now other bodies are not clear, nor are the institutional elaborations that the profession might have to adopt to maintain its regulatory authority. The accounting standard-setting project is increasingly being seen to have achieved ambiguous results, not least in the context of a more commercially orientated profession and a wider environment where the measurement of economic magnitudes can apparently be subject to influence in a more public arena.

Quite active attention has also been given to the appropriate educational and training policies for accountants. The ways in which emerging information-processing technologies might modify the accountant's role have been considered. And, not least in significance, an awareness has emerged of the ways in which major changes in the provision of financial services might put pressure on at least parts of the accountancy profession to re-evaluate their strategic posture vis-à-vis a more turbulent and interdependent outside world.

The accounting agenda has most certainly been in a state of flux. Things which a few people might possibly have dreamed about a few years ago are now starting to happen. Moreover, the issues remaining now seem to be more diverse, more rapidly changing and more explicitly interdependent with events in the world at large. If nothing else, it appears to be an agenda that requires careful thought, perhaps a more analytical and considered approach, and certainly a more strategic and proactive stance. Accounting, it would seem, can no longer be allowed to just happen. Too many things are happening to it.

Considering the Future in the Past

Faced with such difficulties in conceiving the accounting future, it is both an interesting and useful exercise to take a mental voyage into the past to consider the challenge that constructing a future-orientated posture and vision might have provided for accounting colleagues of the past.

For although the magnitude and significance of the items on the accounting agenda might possibly be greater now (something which we are sure the contemporary always proclaim), it is nevertheless interesting to reflect not only on whether accounting has some tendency to ebb and flow between periods of major change and more incremental periods of development but also on the difficulties which the former periods create for adopting a more future-orientated stance.

The period from the late 1960s to the early 1970s, for instance, might also be considered as being one of some turbulence for accounting. Then, too, accounting came into the public eye; questions of accounting regulation first seriously entered the professional agenda; the current programme of accounting standardization was initiated; and many professional firms started to become more self-conscious of the business realities facing their partnerships. Although there are both some similarities and major differences from the present configuration of issues and events, the coming together of a series of seemingly diverse circumstances in a concentrated period of time, and the stimulus this provided for professional reflection and change, is nevertheless interesting in the context of present policy discussions.

Would it, one wonders, have been possible to either predict or outline a possibility for such changes standing in the possibly more peaceful times of the late 1950s or early 1960s? Responding to such a question is not easy, not least because we still lack a thorough evaluation of the changes that did occur in the late 1960s and the reasons for them. But be that as it may, one nevertheless feels that it would certainly have been a most difficult undertaking, requiring an acute awareness of, and sensitivity to, the dynamics of accounting change and the factors that impinge upon it. If nothing else, that should introduce some degree of modesty into present deliberations of the accounting future.

One important reason for the difficulty is that accounting does not just unfold or evolve. It does not have its own internal logic of development, at least as far as generating the most momentous changes in its form is concerned. At times, accounting seemingly changes in a more radical manner. It is as if the path of development is a discontinuous one and many of the key factors implicated in the discontinuities reside outside of the realm of accounting itself. Accounting seemingly responds transformationally to events, incorporating at least some external perturbations as permutations of its own form.

That is something that adds considerably to the difficulty of conceiving of the accounting future. Looking ahead to the accounting that is not requires not only a sensitive understanding of accounting itself, but also an acute insight into external forces that can, rather than must, become implicated in accounting, providing a more active catalyst for change. Seen in such terms, the challenge is to recognize the possibilities rather than the necessities for change, a much more difficult endeavour.

Consider some of the preconditions for the changes that occurred in the late 1960s. They followed a period of growing concern with economic magnitudes and economic calculation in general. Governmental policies towards the economy were becoming more precisely articulated, not least in the context of a range of macro-economic problems. There was a growing desire to know what is, something that was particularly manifest in the related sphere of micro-economic policy making and the formulation of industrial strategies. A more pronounced concern with facts was starting to emerge in policy arenas, fuelled by concerns with planning, regulation and intervention. Crises in particular business sectors reinforced such tendencies. Faced with corporate difficulties, agencies of the state became more interested in knowing the prevailing circumstances and understanding the economic and financial forces at work. Accounting data not only entered into such deliberations but were also seen to be problematic in the process. At least in the eyes of some, accounting started to become a more questionable endeavour at the very time when it might also have been becoming an increasingly significant one.

Such an emerging problematization of the accounting craft was reinforced by other forces at work. A growing public interest in the financial sector not only resulted in a more widespread concern with accounting categories, if not accounting itself, but also played some role in the development of a more significant financial press, a phenomenon that was also encouraged by the growing managerial (and accounting) intensity of many organizations, and a resultant growth of employment advertising.

Other changes were underway in the corporate sector, in part resulting from the growing significance and activity of the financial sector, the government's concern with industrial efficiency and the rationales for economies of scale, and the development of financial strategies of corporate growth and a resultant development of new financial practices, including that of the contested takeover bid. Industrial reorganization was leading to a period of mergers and acquisitions, something that resulted not only in a more acute awareness of the need for financial skills in enterprises but also in more explicit appeals to financial and accounting data in the public decision making arena.

No doubt other factors were also at work. Already, however, enough has been said to provide some insight into at least some of the pressures that were to play a key role in providing a basis for an accounting discontinuity. Agencies of the state started to develop a more questioning stance towards accounting. Not least because of the development of a more active financial media, the more problematic implication of accounting in industrial restructuring was brought into the public domain. With the development of a more systematic and economically rational stance towards corporate strategic decision making in at least some companies, such problems were also of concern to the industrial community as users rather than just providers of accounting information. All be it that they emanated from a diverse but interrelated complex of institutions and issues, a basis was nevertheless created for accounting to be questioned and for that questioning to result in change.

Not dissimilar circumstances have surrounded the functioning of one of the institutions of the new accounting — the Accounting Standards Committee. If we consider the fluctuating history of the inflation accounting initiative, for instance, again we see accounting embedded in a complex of factors that range from the economic through the social and the political. Although it still remains ambiguous whether the initial move was taken by the profession or the government, there is perhaps less doubt that one of the important significances associated with the early debates was one of innovation itself. At a time when the initial enthusiasm and goodwill for the standardization project might have been waning, the new proposal was meant to be a sign that the profession was prepared to look at more basic issues in accounting rather than merely attending to surface manifestations. But there can be no doubt that the innovators, whoever they might have been, failed to appreciate the different issues and agendas with which the seemingly technical proposals thereafter became involved.

Within government circles, not only did these proposals interface with the administration of taxation but they also were subjected to shifting interpretations within the context of changes in macroeconomic policy. At first they were seen as a form of indexation, something that was not perceived with favour at that time, although it could well have been a little earlier. Later the idea of an adjusted account was more positively regarded in the midst of debates on industrial strategy, being seen as something that could enable a more precise revelation of the lack of investment in British manufacturing industry. Such diverse and shifting influences even resulted in conflicting perspectives on inflation accounting within the Whitehall establishment itself.

On the corporate side, the debates were active at a time of heightened trade union power, and some commentators assigned inflation accounting a particular significance in the context of more politically orientated debates on the management of corporate surplus declaration. But the corporate stance was not a uniform one. The differential impacts of different inflation accounting proposals led to an intense and competitive lobbying by sectors interested in the wider consequences of the precise impacts on their financial reports. No doubt to the dismay and surprise of the innovators, accounting became a much disputed phenomenon and one subject to analysis by competing bodies of theoretical knowledge that until then had had a more equivocal relationship to the practice of the accounting craft. In such a context of discord and disagreement, questions of professional governance and representation also entered into the inflation accounting debate.

All too clearly the complex and troublesome path of development followed by the inflation accounting debate was not anticipated by those initially seeking a more technical reform of the accounting craft. They had not conceived that such a technical change could be located in a wider nexus of relationships, many of which were conflicting, had no *a priori* relationship to accounting and were themselves shifting phenomena. Accounting had been seen primarily in just technical terms. Not only was the vision of the accounting future thus a limited one but it would also appear that accounting itself was simply not recognized as a potentially influential form of social practice which could, and often did, have wider ramifications and consequences. With the benefit of hindsight, a purely technical view of accounting, although of some importance for guiding the technical elements of the debate, has to be seen as only a partial perspective and certainly one that provided little basis for appreciating the range of possible future policy implications that could stem from such an accounting change.

Seen in such terms, the inflation accounting episode, like the more widespread debate and changes in the late 1960s, has some relevance when considering the possibilities for a more future-orientated view of accounting. At the very least, it helps to illuminate the difficulty of gaining an adequate understanding of the processes at work in accounting change, let alone of predicting the path of accounting development. Accounting policy makers in the late 1960s and early 1970s could not have done the latter and neither can we now.

Such a conclusion must not be taken as an incentive for inaction, however, or for neglecting the need for greater sensitivity of thought. It does not condone the partiality of past views or reinforce the status quo. For although the accounting past is undoubtedly clouded by very real uncertainties, such short outlines of some important sagas in accounting's recent past suggest that even if prediction was and is impossible, it is possible to advance an intelligent explanation of at least some of the processes through which accounting became what it was not. Moreover, in the present context, such an intelligibility, imperfect though it may at present be, has a contemporary as well as a historical significance. For in allowing us to ground our understanding of accounting in the wider circumstances in which it functions, it can play a useful role in sensitizing us to important aspects of the accounting environment and creating an awareness of the wider social and economic transformations with which accounting can become intertwined.

Particular readings of the past can thus help us to perceive at least some of the forces out of which the future might be constructed. At the very least, they can introduce an element of dynamics into a subject that is so often seen in purely static terms: accounting can be seen in the process of becoming. They can place the technical in the context of the institutions out of which it emerges. They can destabilize the obviousness of the present, illustrating accounting when it was not as it now is, and thereby enable a possibility of conceiving of accounting as it might become. And they can provide an insight into some of the complex ways in which accounting, positively and often surprisingly, emerges, thereby enabling a more questioning stance to be adopted towards the views of those who emphasize the musts and the imperatives of the accounting craft. Accounting now has forms and functions that people could not have imagined it might, let alone must, have; and no doubt it will come to be something that is not reflected in the domain of today's necessities.

Of equal significance, such a view of accounting's past is suggestive of methodologies and ways of conceiving of the accounting future. If it is not possible to predict, that does not imply that it is futile to explore the future in order to develop a more proactive stance. Attempts can usefully be made to explicate at least some of the institutional and environmental contexts and issues in which accounting might become embedded. Being fully aware that many of the factors that powerfully impinge on accounting reside outside of the control of accountants, it is nevertheless possible to attempt to conceive of a range of different configurations of feasible circumstances and the implications that these might have for accounting. Just such a view provided the basis for the Understanding a Changing Environment Group's use of scenario analysis, an approach explained more fully elsewhere in this volume.

Some Factors Involved in Accounting Change

Recognizing the potential for sensitizing and learning, and realizing the importance of improving our understanding of the forces that can and do put accounting into motion, it can be of some value to reflect a little more on some of the themes that might emerge out of a consideration of accounting as it has come to be in the United Kingdom.

An Uninevitable Path

Accounting has not just evolved. Over time it has been subject to more radical transformations. No general principles, be they overt or hidden from view, have guided its development. Accounting has responded in a more positive way to external as well as internal pressures and circumstances, internalizing into itself residues of events and disruptions in the contexts in which it operates.

Such a view of accounting requires that particular attention needs to be given to the economic, social and political environments in which it operates. Accounting needs to be seen as a more open phenomenon. Consideration must be given to the particular institutional arenas in which accounting comes to function and to how these can create contexts in which accounting comes to change. Rather than adopting a generalized view of an accounting potential, a more specific stance must be adopted which enables an appreciation of how accounting, as an influential form of economic calculation, comes to be intertwined with specific issues, problems and debates.

The specificity rather than inevitability of accounting can perhaps best be seen in a comparative setting. For accounting seemingly has come to have a very different significance in the British national context than elsewhere in the industrialized world. The United Kingdom has invested heavily in the accounting craft and in accountants themselves, possibly having one of the highest accountants per capita ratios in the Western world. As the deliberaions on accounting harmonization in the European Community illustrate, the British have assigned quite distinct roles to accounting, have utilized accounting skills in a wide diversity of domains, and have attributed a quite distinct social significance and sphere of autonomy to the practitioners of the accounting craft and their institutional forums. In Britain, for instance, an accounting training is perceived to provide a much more generalized awareness. We also tend more readily to attribute particular economic significance to accounting magnitudes, not least in a performance context. And we assume a similarity between an accounting aptitude and the skills of corporate financial management that has few equivalents elsewhere.

If nothing else, such contrasts demonstrate that there is no inevitability to the specific form of accounting that we have. It does not arise unproblematically from an industrialized society or even a capitalist one. A national manifestation of accounting seemingly reflects quite specific national forms, institutions and modes of functioning.

Therefore if accounting is to be made intelligible, not least in a policy-orientated manner, a view of the accounting actuality needs

to infuse our awareness of it rather than a conception of an inevitable phenomenon having a potential that is seemingly independent of the precise modes in which it functions at any particular
point in time and space. Rather than just appealing to a rationale of
accounting providing relevant information for decision making, for
instance, if we are to understand how such a generalized ideal is
implicated in accounting transformations we need to appreciate the
shifting conceptions of relevancy, the factors which induce these to
change, and the nature of the contexts in which appeals are made to
such a generalized ideal as a basis for change. Relevancy *per se*
provides few insights into such specific processes. Similar difficulties
apply to general conceptions of accountability which also are often
put forward as explanations of the disruptions that occur in accounting. Significant though such a conception may at times be as a
facilitator of accounting change, its very ambiguity provides few
possibilities for appreciating the ways in which it comes to intersect
with particular accountings at particular periods of time. Like that
for relevancy, such an understanding also requires a much more
focused view.

Appreciations of accounting therefore need to be grounded ones
rather than ones that appeal to generalized absolutes. Consideration
must be given to what accounting is and how it might come to be
different, rather than only to what accounting should, ought or must
be. While significant in an ethical and normative sense, such
concerns with imperatives seemingly provide only a partial insight
into how accounting actually operates, having only an equivocal and
ambiguous relationship with the actual practice of the craft.

External Influences on Accounting

In trying to understand accounting, particular attention needs to be
given to appreciating how it responds to external crises or major
perturbations in the environments in which it functions. For an
awareness of the accounting past suggests that it is just such events
that result in significant increases in the extent of economic calculation and resultant ramifications for accounting itself.

A professionalized accounting as we now know it emerged
amidst the bankruptcy crises that came with the depression at the
end of the nineteenth century. Professional accounting came to have
its first significant associations with accounting within the enterprise
in the context of the First World War. Working as agents of the
state at a time when there were concerns with increasing the
efficiency of the use of the scarce resources available in a wartime
economy and addressing accusations of war profiteering, accountants

started to see an involvement with 'trade' as a potentially more reputable task.

Industrial restructuring in the depressed times of the 1920s and 1930s brought accountants into the senior management cadre of industrial enterprises. After the Second World War, it was the state that started to appeal to accountants as agents of industrial change, seemingly able to play a role in increasing the economic rationality of managerial action at a time when emphasis was being placed on economic growth and the enhancement of the competitive position of the British industrial sector.

Such tendencies have also been manifest more recently. Although the origins of the appeals to a more elaborated economic and accounting calculus have been diverse, ranging from issues of industrial relations, through continued concerns with industrial restructuring, to present-day political concerns with relocating the boundary between the public and the private spheres of economic action, accounting seemingly has continued to flourish at times of major policy discontinuity when renewed appeals are made for a new domain of the economically factual and the means for its wider dissemination.

Accounting at such times gets tied up with interests in making different phenomena visible to different people or groups. In such contexts accounting has a potential for becoming involved with very disparate agendas, some of which have no relationship to the accounting past or any *a priori* relationship to accounting *per se*. Possibilities can be created for accounting to be transformed by pressures emanating from outside its own spheres of influence. Stemming from a desire to modify, regulate or change, such concerns with new ways of perceiving and knowing can create an interest in the construction of a sphere of the potentially economically governable on the basis of appeals to a legitimate mode of enhancing economic visibility and the flexible and adaptable calculus that is accounting.

Although at times sudden transformations and crises can have a significance in their own right, on other occasions they provide the catalyst by which more long standing trends and tensions are brought to bear on accounting. Such was possibly the case in the late 1960s. Important though a series of quite specific corporate and accounting scandals may have been in mobilizing accounting change, they nevertheless need to be appreciated in the context of more long standing economic and institutional developments which had a latent potential to influence accounting. In such instances highly specific events can sometimes help to convert trends into crises. In a policy context, however, that difference is a significant one. Responses to such crises should ideally be cognisant of, and informed by, a knowledge of the underlying trends. One senses that this is not always the case.

Accounting and the State

As should now be clear, accounting has tended to have a close and mutually supportive relationship with the state. The profession developed on the basis of a legal requirement for audit and eventually achieved a legal monopoly in its provision. It also has a long history of service to the state as a provider of legitimate economic information, something that continues to the present day as governmental agencies seek to diffuse a wider economic consciousness throughout their organizations. As such an example illustrates, the relationship with the state is by means a one-sided one. The modern state has itself emerged and developed on the basis of rationalized practices of management, including those involving accounting. Moreover, it has used accounting information not only as a basis for its collection of revenues but also as a means for operationalizing more widespread strategies in areas as diverse as industrial restructuring, industrial relations, and the regulation of specific activities and sectors. Accounting and the state have in some senses been mutually constitutive of each other.

Of course the profession generally does not view the relationship in such terms, even though it repeatedly acts on the axis of relationship with the state. Rather, it tends to have a view of an original professional autonomy that has been and still is threatened by the interventionist policies of the state. At any specific point in time that might be a useful way of characterizing the relationship because debates can take place over which particular functions and activities should reside in the realms of the profession and the state. Seen in terms of a longer time perspective, however, the dominant view is one that ignores many of the processes by which accounting emerged to be as it now is.

Although the interventionist view is an understandable one and possibly, in the context of a need to mobilize discussions and concerns, a necessary one also, its partiality nevertheless needs to be recognized when a more future-orientated perspective is adopted. For the state has been an important influence on accounting and it is difficult to envisage that changing.

Accounting has Repeatedly Become What it Was Not

A newly professionalized accountancy provided a context in which a group of practitioners often more concerned with bankruptcy

administration than audit could become more widely recognized as
auditors *per se*. Acting initially in the service of a wartime state, these
auditors started to become involved with cost accounting, something
until then deemed to be more the province of clerks than professionals. Industrial reorganization and the development of large
modern corporate forms thereafter provided an opportunity for this
involvement with the intricacies of trade to develop into a more
comprehensive concern with financial management. Working on the
axis between the state and the business enterprise, the British
accountant became involved with tax administration, corporate
investigations and other regulatory concerns. In more recent times,
the private sector accountant and auditor has entered the field of
public sector accounting, something hitherto of seemingly little
interest. And the increasing involvement with managerial and
financial matters has provided opportunities for more explicit
associations with systems analysis and design, management consultancy and general financial services work.

Accounting has therefore occupied a fluid and shifting domain.
Whatever accounting was, it seemingly always has had a tendency
to become something different.

As has already been stated, such shifts were neither inevitable
nor reflective of factors intrinsic to the accounting task. For the
British accountant now performs a range of activities more broadly
defined than those exercised by many colleagues elsewhere. Tax
administration is not obviously an accounting task, since it is often
performed by lawyers or others elsewhere. The accountant has no
natural right to be involved in corporate financial management,
however obvious the relationship might seem. In most other
countries that is perceived to be the sphere of other experts with very
different training and bodies of knowledge — the business economist,
the general management expert or the finance specialist. Similarly for
today's accountant's concern with management systems and public
sector work. No gradual process of the realization of some implicit
accounting potential is at work. If only because of contrasting
experiences elsewhere, a more positive and proactive view is needed
to account for what the accountant now does and what he or she
might do in the future.

In part, the explanations for the shifting domain of accounting
reside in the specific nexus of institutions and policy arenas with
which the British accountant has become involved. However,
particular consideration also needs to be given to the fact that, unlike
elsewhere, there have been few, if any, alternative sources of
expertise in the British context, at least until relatively recently. No
early investment was made in systematic managerial and financial
training, as was made in the United States. British universities have

not produced a cadre of applied economists trained in the knowledge relevant to business analysis, as in Germany, Scandinavia, the Netherlands, Italy and elsewhere. The British accountant has had the quite enviable position of having relatively few competing sources of expertise, a factor which historically must have played an important role in determining his or her pre-eminent position.

Such external factors most likely provide only a partial insight into accounting's shifting terrain in the United Kingdom, however. Accountants themselves would appear to have been, and indeed quite obviously still are, a quite proactive group that has not confused what is with what might be. They have not been noted for failing to recognize and act upon new opportunities for both individual and professional mobilization. A culture of professional entrepreneurship appears to have pervaded the accounting community. As such, this appears to be something that contrasts with the situation prevailing in the British legal community, where a more gentlemanly and sedate ambience would not appear to have been prevalent until of late, and that in the communities of industrial management and engineering, which perhaps did not have the wider social recognition that is so important for effective action in the British context.

From the perspective of a more future-orientated view of accounting, such an analysis of the factors implicated in accounting's shifting terrain are of some interest. The lack of inevitability might be suggestive of the roles that can be played by policy making and choices. That domains for professional action are not given but emerge from a competitive stance, albeit one that is much modified by the institutional context and the perceptions and expectations of significant others, reinforces the role which a more proactive stance might play. For accounting would not appear to be something that is wholly determined from without. A sphere for determined action most clearly does exist.

Accounting and the Skills of Accountants

Many such tactical moves into pastures new reflected the skills, aspirations and energies of individual accountants. Knowledge seemingly has not been deemed to be a significant constraint on occupational mobility, at least in the past. The accountant has repeatedly done what he or she has not done before, creating an expertise and reputation after entering new fields rather than acquiring them beforehand, a process that is still evident.

No doubt helped by a lack of effective competition, the British accountant has been one of the few who by reason of training and experience could claim some awareness of matters financial and even managerial, rather than purely accounting techniques. Such tendencies, no doubt, have also been furthered by both individual mobility aspirations and the emergent social position of the accountant in British society. Accounting had less of a history of professional status. It most likely often attracted the aspirant rather than those who had a more established position, enabling the personal enthusiasms, energies and ambitions of the members of the accounting community, both individually and collectively, to shape not only their own personal life spaces but, in so doing, also influence the domain that was seen to be accounting itself.

Such a fluidity of domain and a flexibility of individual temperament has most likely also played a more significant role in enabling the accounting community to keep abreast of new developments than have the activities of the professional institutes. At least until recently, the latter have often adopted a more reactive stance, recognizing what accounting has come to be rather than more proactively sketching a map of what it might become. In areas such as the impact of office technology, and now that of information processing technology, the increasing formalization of the knowledge bases of auditing and the incorporation of more systematic and often economics-based bodies of knowledge into financial management, one is tempted to look for the sources of innovation residing in the proactive initiative of individuals rather than in the deliberations and pronouncements of the institutional embodiments of the community as a whole.

Once again, it is all too clear that there are no inevitabilities associated with such a pattern of development and modification, as the experiences of other and perhaps less successful occupational groupings might demonstrate. Individual actions need to be in line with wider developments and the expectations which at least some significant others (including those in the professional community) might hold or might be prepared to hold of the accounting craft. There can also be other sources of change, including some institutionalized ones in the professional community. For, as we have seen already, certain realignments require a collective response. Moreover, some of the environmental facilitators of such an individualized and proactive response can themselves also change.

The lack of effective competition, for instance, is something that is clearly changing, not least in the area of industrial accounting and financial management. Albeit that developments are still slow, there has nevertheless been a growing investment in business education in the British higher educational sector, and individuals with Master of Business Administration (MBA) qualifications are now directly entering financial executive positions in the corporate and financial sectors. Although the scale of change is such that competitive professionals cannot possibly occupy all financial positions in industrial and commercial organizations, there is already some evidence that they are occupying some of the more visible and significant ones in the larger enterprises and in the City. This is something that is common, indeed the norm, in other industrialized countries, but is equally something that would have been difficult to imagine in the British context even a short while ago. Surely, it was thought, a finance director *must* be a professionally qualified accountant. But as accountants themselves have so frequently demonstrated, 'must' is a term that resides uncomfortably in the accounting arena.

A number of trends lie behind such developments, factors that are, or should be, of concern to an occupational group that has relied on more individualized, experiential and proactive modes of responding to and creating change.

For one thing, the organization of the industrial finance function has changed, increasingly adopting, explicitly or implicitly, the American model of a division between the accounting, controllership and treasury roles. The professional accountant still remains admirably qualified for the first role, although that is no longer, perhaps, the most significant of the three. The other two roles increasingly require a wider knowledge base, one that might be acquired by an accountant, but not necessarily so, and one that is certainly available to other experts and occupational groups. A new basis for competition has therefore been created.

Until recently, much of the accountant's knowledge had not been formalized. Experiential learning was more important was than a systematic exposure to formal and analytical bodies of knowledge, something that itself not only restricted competition but also bestowed an aura of mystic on the resultant expertise. That is changing, however, for reasons that have little or nothing to do with accounting itself. In many areas of finance and management more systematic bodies of knowledge have arisen in recent decades. Let it be clear that these in no way eliminate the need for experience, intuition and entrepreneurial flair. But they do nevertheless increasingly constrain the possibilities for entry into many financial positions. Modern industrial and commercial bureaucracies worldwide have come to be based, in part, on more rationalized bodies of knowledge and practices. As a result, the language of management has changed and is becoming a more structured and specialized one. Moreover, a complex and turbulent environment often requires more than just intuition and experience to formulate strategies and tactics that can cope with intricate patterns of interdependencies and significant second-order effects. Analysis is also required, and often analyses of quite specialized kinds. Finally, many of the new artifacts of the managerial and financial world, including some of the newer financial instruments, are themselves based on more formal and analytical bodies of knowledge. Dealing with them still requires judgement and flair; of that there is no doubt. Increasingly, however, it also requires more specialized skills and understanding.

Such tendencies are also likely to become more significant in the modern world for other, more general, reasons. Increasingly, a wider social expectation is arising which demands of experts, or those who claim expertise, a rational and legitimate basis of knowledge rather than one which appeals to more traditional sources of authority. In the United Kingdom, perhaps, such changes are still less evident since many sectors of the establishment still have a more equivocal relationship to modern bases of knowledge. But changes are nevertheless underway, as is evidenced by experiences in other occupational and professional areas. To the extent that such tendencies continue to develop, experience and reputation alone may no longer be sufficient bases for the exercising of not only the expertise itself but also the wider authority and power that so often goes with it.

Indeed, the accountancy profession has already had to reflect on the implications of such changes, if only indirectly. In accounting standards setting, for instance, the potential for a wider professional regulatory role has increasingly resulted in a consideration of, if not a questioning of, the bases for such an authority. While claims of professional experience and judgement might have been sufficient in the past, more attention is now having to be given to alternative bases of legitimacy, including not only representational ones but also the role of knowledge.

So although this is an area where change remains gradual, there is nevertheless some reason to think that the accounting community might have to consider the future relationships between individual-ized expertise and a more formal view of a relevant body of knowledge, and between a reputation based on experience coupled with an entrepreneurial flair for the new and one that appeals to an authority grounded in part on more rational and analytical bases.

Structuring a Context for Exploring the Accounting Future

Being aware of such themes and tendencies, the question arose as to how best to structure a consideration of the accounting future, not least in respect of the activities of the Understanding a Changing

Environment Group. Although there were undoubtedly a number of approaches available for this, the above analysis was suggestive of some quite distinct possibilities for shaping the context for the Group's deliberations, its methodological approach to the future, some specific issues which were worthy of its attention and, not least in significance, the nature of the Group itself.

Context

Recognizing the extent to which accounting changes are embedded in a wider economic, social and institutional context, it was important for the Group to first appreciate some of the changing elements in that context and the possibilities that are perceived for its future direction. This the Group did, paying particular attention to those factors which were already seen to be in the course of development and those where genuine uncertainties, disagreements and options existed, particularly where these seemed to have a potential relevance, however indirect, for the future path of accounting itself.

Specific attention was given to a consideration of economic and social trends. Emphasis was placed not only on the shifting path of the British economy but also on the increasing internationalization of the economic domain. Consideration was given to the changing structure of the economy, the evolving place within it of the financial sector and the possible location of the British economy in the wider patterns of international developments. Social changes were also discussed explicitly , with particular consideration being given to the changing nature of industrial relations and the implications which this might have for economic performance and management.

Rather than just considering these changes in isolation, an attempt was made to discuss their accounting relevance. In part this was done by continually emphasizing the extent to which such economic and social factors were implicated, not only in the shifting nature of accounting in the past, but also in so many of the accounting problems and possibilities of today. Aware of such an interdependency, the Group attempted to move its perspective forward in time to at least ponder the possibilities for the future.

Undoubtedly the discussions of the Group are already in need of some revision. That is implicit in the nature of the task, given the uncertain and dynamic nature of the world in which we live. And that is something which is at least suggestive of the need for a future-orientated stance to be a continual one rather than something that is only rarely adopted. Be that as it may, however, the Group's particular considerations of the accounting context were helpful in locating accounting in its wider setting, in providing an early emphasis on the crucial interdependencies between accounting and the non-accounting, and in stretching the imaginations of the members of the Group such that they could at least consider some possibilities for quite significant change.

Method

Consideration also had to be given to delineating a stance towards a discussion of the future and the appropriate methodologies for realizing it. Recognizing the lack of inevitability that characterizes the accounting past, being aware of the important roles that have been played by discontinuities, and noting the uncertainty surrounding key factors that could help to shape the accounting future, prediction *per se* was of little help in providing a basis on which consideration might be given to what accounting might become. Emphasis was therefore placed on delineating a number of viable scenarios of the future, each of which has a certain credibility and all of which provide a questioning and stimulating arena in which futures can be conceived and deliberated. The scenario approach has been explicitly discussed in an earlier chapter, along with the outline scenarios that emerged from the discussions of the Group.

Such a way of conceiving the future was significant, not only in terms of the particular scenarios which emerged, but also because of the type of orientation which it gave to other, more general, discussions of the Group. Rather than emphasizing what would be, an impossible task in the dynamic world in which we live, the scenario approach helped the Group focus on possibilities, on understanding the process of change, and on appreciating the ways in which quite complex configurations of circumstances can come to impinge on accounting. Instead of pointing to the delineation of an inevitable future, such an approach is more suggestive of a need for sound intelligence, careful analysis and a consideration of options. Compared with a forecast-based approach, it offers a means for considering the future that is more compatible with a proactive policy-orientated stance. It was the latter which was the concern of the Understanding a Changing Environment Group.

Issues for Analysis

The mode of analysis of accounting outlined earlier was also suggestive of some issues and topics which might be both important and conducive to reflection on future options and constraints.

Although numerous possibilities undoubtedly exist, particular consideration was given to the following:

- the functioning and changing nature of the professional firm;
- the position of the accountant in industry;
- the impacts which new information processing technologies could have;
- the accounting standard-setting process;
- the position of the accountancy profession in the context of the wider regulation of financial institutions and transactions.

Reports on each of these more focused discussions have been given in earlier chapters.

Although other significant topics come to mind, some of the most important of these, such as the relationship between the profession and the state, forms of professional governance, and questions related to education and training, naturally infused many, if not all, the other deliberations, thereby providing a useful cross-hatching of issues and concerns.

The Nature of the Discussion Process

The overall process by which the Understanding a Changing Environment Group attempted to consider the accounting future was both a particular and a partial one. Nevertheless, it provided a stimulating framework within which discussion could take place about the accounting that has yet to come.

Although the official brief was always one of talking about the future, it was hardly surprising that much of the discussion focused on current problems and concerns. The future-orientated context nevertheless had a very real significance. It facilitated not only a more frank and open discussion but also one that was strategically, as well as tactically, orientated. The emphasis on the future provided a basis on which the present could be related to the future, and out of that process emerged a series of more questioning and provocative deliberations.

Considerations such as the latter serve to emphasize that the overall effectiveness of any such assignment is crucially dependent on the particular composition of the group engaged upon it. In this respect the Understanding a Changing Environment Group was fortunate. A lot was gained by having as members senior and influential people from both within and without the accountancy profession. Discussions were almost invariably both animated and informed. Indeed, they often resulted in a richness of insight that is only very partially reflected in the final reports and summaries. Much of the overall benefit resided in the members of the Group themselves and for this reason alone it was of some importance that the Group contained people who could diffuse more widely the understandings and insights gained. Often, actual decision makers or potential decision makers do not take part in such processes of future orientated discussion and scenario generation. On this occasion, it could be argued, at least some of them did and the exercise was all the better for it.

The Present Moving Towards the Future

It is in the nature of things that the future is emergent in the present. This was no less the case for the Understanding a Changing Environment Group. The accounting agenda was a shifting one during the course of its deliberations; new issues became apparent; somewhat different worries were articulated; new emphases were given to more long standing issues.

Some of these emergent concerns have been mentioned in the reports of the Group's discussions. Others concerns have perhaps been given less explicit considerations, however. Given this, it is useful to comment on a number of such developing issues, not least because there is some probability that they will continue to infuse and shape accounting discussions and actions.

The Internationalization of Accounting

The growing internationalization of accounting is one such issue. The Group gave some consideration to the international nature of the major auditing firms, the increasing significance of financial controls in multinational business corporations, and at least some of the implications for British accounting and its professional institutions of the globalization of the financial markets. On reflection, however, and with the benefit of hindsight, it might be that the implications of these and other related international developments were not pursued sufficiently.

The emphasis, perhaps quite naturally, still tended to be on British accounting. Yet British accounting is now starting to be subjected to an increasing number of non-British influences, and the probability is that these will continue and most likely grow, not just in the context of supranational regulation and standardization but also through the influences of an increasingly autonomous and international financial sector and a post-1992 European economy.

Although, undoubtedly, the national setting will continue to influence how at least some international influences and pressures are interpreted and applied, the probability is that the United Kingdom will increasingly become an importer as well as an exporter of accounting and related knowledges and techniques. This will not just apply to the practices of financial accounting and corporate disclosure, but also to modes of financial regulation, to audit methods, which in the larger firms are already subject to international standardization emanating from the United States, to approaches to the financial control of the larger enterprise, and to professional education, training and certification.

Already conscious of these developments, the professional institutes are in the process of mobilizing their intelligence gathering and lobbying mechanisms in at least some of these areas. But one still wonders whether the full potential and implications of some of the internationalizing forces for change have been fully appreciated.

The Shifting Knowledge Bases of Accounting

Quite considerable emphasis has already been placed on the changing knowledge bases underlying accounting and the Group was very conscious of this fact in its deliberations. In the area of accounting standard-setting, for instance, increasing appeals are being made to more formal bodies of knowledge and the probability is that this trend will continue to develop. Indeed, the professional institutes are themselves furthering it, partly in response to the increasing complexity of the problems being dealt with and partly because of the growing pressures for accountants not only to do, but also to articulate their rationales for doing.

Financial management in the larger enterprise is subject to similar pressures. Increasingly, more rationalized and formal bodies of knowledge are being incorporated into the task of the financial executive, influencing not only what he or she does but also the language, categories and perspectives that are appealed to during the course of quite regular work activities. With the increasing involvement of accountants in general management activities, they too are having to grapple with the greater knowledge intensity of the modern management task, at least in the larger firms.

Auditing is certainly not exempt from such pressures. Moreover, in the governmental domain the increasing involvement of accounting and accountants will in all probability also result in growing pressures for an explication of the rationales, presumptions and logic underlying accounting practices, particularly when such practices are analysed from the perspective of more formalized bodies of economic reasoning.

Many members of the profession, are already well aware of these tendencies. Indeed they have already created quite visible problems for the profession, the inflation accounting debate being only one quite specific example.

Within the profession, one factor that has some probability of increasing the extent to which more focused questions are raised abut the state of accounting knowledge is the increasing educational basis of its members. Accounting is increasingly a graduate profession. Indeed, in recent years it has recruited some of the best minds into its ranks, the full implications of which have yet to materialize. Moreover, the profession is increasingly moving into areas of activity which are more influenced by formalized bases of knowledge, that of management consultancy being not least in significance. Already, this is resulting in debates and indeed tensions about the appropriateness of different knowledges and the requirements for new ones within the larger professional firms. It is difficult to envisage that in time these pressures will not infuse wider professional deliberations.

Indeed, such concerns are already influencing the professional agenda, both with respect to educational policies and the articulation of a perspective vis-à-vis the role of accounting research. Such interests emerge in part from some of the factors outlined above but one senses that they also are being pursued because of an increasing awareness of the emergent competition from other expert groups in the occupational markets in which accountants operate.

Although it is difficult to delineate any precise set of implications stemming from these developments, the probability is that more and more attention will need to be given to them. And this will not be an easy task for the accountancy profession. In the past it has devoted relatively little effort to explicating, formalizing and propagating its interests in knowledge. Its training activities have tended to be based on those of a craft, emphasizing experiential skills and learning by doing. Examinations and their contents have had a somewhat loose relationship to the tasks of the accountant. And at times, including quite recently, at least some sectors of the profession have chosen to distance themselves from more explicit concerns with the structures of accounting knowledge. Many of these perspectives and practices of the past are quite understandable, particularly when seen in the contexts in which they emerged. That, however, need not imply that they provide a continuing basis for action in a different world that might be the future.

Commercial and Professional Interests

The growing salience of commercial and competitive pressures in the accountancy profession did enter into the Group's discussions; there was a consciousness of the growing tensions that this creates. Mention was made of the increasing pressures that result from this within the professional firm, only very few of which ever enter the public domain. The full range of possible implications of being in what American journalists now call the 'audit business' was not fully developed, however, most likely quite understandably so. Not only is this an area where it is difficult to articulate publicly what is at stake, it is also one in which many of the pressures are still emergent and often subject to quite conflicting influences.

There is little doubt, however, that questions relating to the balance between professional and commercial concerns will play a significant role in future accounting deliberations, be that explicitly or implicitly. Some of them provide a background to debates on both accounting standardization and financial regulation. They have already influenced the structure of the firms that constitute the profession quite considerably, and no doubt will continue to do so. Although the profession itself is only now consciously focusing on its strategic posture vis-à-via the future, many of its member firms have long since done so for sound commercial reasons and have changed their profile of activities as a result.

Even in official circles in the United Kingdom, accounting is increasingly coming to be seen and regulated as if it is an industrial sector. Indeed, that very language is starting to be used. Increasing emphasis is being placed on the size of the British investment in accounting, its employment and wealth creating roles, the significant part it plays in the market for highly skilled labour and, more recently, its export potential. Already, such a view of accounting is starting to influence policies towards the profession and if such trends continue they will certainly raise interesting questions related to the balance between the industrial and the regulatory roles of the profession.

Moving into the Future

Although the accounting past and present have been much influenced by external factors, accounting is not only determined from without. A key requirement for understanding the path of accounting change also lies in recognizing the need to relate the accounting present not only to past circumstances but also to the aspirations and actions of members of the accounting community, both individually and collectively. External circumstances have shaped, constrained and directed the nature of the accounting craft and its professional manifestation, but they have rarely, if ever, determined it. Spheres for both individual and collective action have been maintained such that accounting as we now know it reflects an intertwining of pressure from without and the exercising of choice from within.

It is the positive role that can be played by the use of discretion and choice that makes the type of exercise undertaken by the Understanding a Changing Environment Group one of some importance. There is every reason to believe that a more conscious and well thought out view of the future can only help the accountancy profession to articulate a more proactive, and possibly more influential, set of aspirations and possible courses of action.

At times when change is great the need for such a future-orientated policy stance is also great. There is a greater need to appreciate the nature of the forces at work and the ways in which they might intersect with accounting practice. It becomes more important to have a clearer understanding of professional aims and aspirations so that these can also infuse and, hopefully, influence the discussion of possible options and the selection of preferred modes of action. For when the accounting context is in a state of flux, without such a more informed and proactive perspective it is easier for pressures from without to impinge on accounting in the terms of other interests rather than those of accountants themselves.

The deliberations of the Understanding a Changing Environment Group were temporary and their reports and conclusions undoubtedly partial and reflective of the concerns prevailing at the time they were articulated. If the accounting context remains a turbulent one, as most definitely seems to be the case, there thus remains a continuing need for the profession to consider the future and the forces out of which it is created if it is to maintain, let alone enhance, its sphere of effective influence. There is likely to be a growing need for intelligence on the forces that can impinge on accounting. It will become more important to invest in understanding the, often quite complex, processes out of which accounting change emerges. The importance of informed delineation of options for the future can only increase.

Such a view of the requirements for a future responsible and influential accountancy profession suggest that at least some members of the profession, be they in individual firms or representative of the profession at large, will need to give continuing thought to how the profession can realize, sustain and develop these capabilities. Given a clear probability that the management of change will become of more, rather than less, importance, even more attention will need to be given to locating the key resources for doing this within the professional community and to ensuring that its senior representatives are both informed and creative in a policy making sense. If the discussions of the Understanding a Changing Environment Group only achieve a greater awareness of such needs, they will have achieved a lot.

Appendix 1

Membership of the Understanding a Changing Environment Group

Convenor:

Professor A.G. Hopwood,
London School of
Economics and
Political Science

Office-holders of the
ICAEW during the period
of the study:

A. Hardcastle
B. Jenkins
D. Boothman
A. Green
F.E. Worsley

Secretary of the ICAEW:

E.J.D. Warne

Chairman of the Research
Board:

C. Swinson

Director of Research:

Professor B.V. Carsberg

Technical Director:

G.B. Mitchell

Secretary to Group:

W.S. Turley

Members: J.H. Bowman,
Price Waterhouse

Mrs S. Brown,
Department of Trade and
Industry

Members:

A.R.J. Calvert, Esso (UK) plc	J.A. Cope, Member of Parliament
Professor D.J. Cooper, University of Manchester Institute of Science and Technology	A.A. Duguid, Department of Trade and Industry
C.J. Farrow, Bank of England	Mrs S. I. Gompels, Chartered Accountant
B.A. Gould, Member of Parliament	J.J. Hanley, Member of Parliament
J.D. Hanson, Arthur Andersen & Co.	N.P. Hepworth, Director Chartered Institute of Public Finance and Accountancy
E.A. Kench, E.A. Kench & Co.	H. Liesner, Department of Trade and Industry
Ms S.V. Masters, Peat Marwick McLintock & Co.	M.J. Page, University of Southampton
M.J. Parry, Chartered Accountant	R.C.L. Perry, Coopers & Lybrand
J. Reeve, Mercantile House Holdings plc	P.J. Rutteman, Arthur Young
D.J. Taylor, Robson Taylor & Co.	Mrs R.P. Thorne, Habitat, Mothercare Plc

Appendix 1

Members:

S.W. Treadgold,	R.G. Willott,
Department of Trade	Spicer & Oppenheim
and Industry	

Some changes in membership did take place as the study
progressed and the above list includes all those who were members
of the UCEG for any part of the two-year period of the study.

Appendix 2

Meetings of the Understanding a Changing Environment Group

Speaker(s)	*Subject*
Sir James Ball, London Business School	The development of the UK economy during the next fifteen years
Terry Ward, Cambridge University	
Professor George Bain, University of Warwick	Social futures
Professor Peter Townsend, University of Bristol	
Pierre Wack	Planning for the longer term and the use of scenarios
Eric Kench, EA Kench & Co.	Future development of professional practice
David Taylor, Robson Taylor	
Bob Willott, Spicer & Oppenheim	

Andrew Calvert, ESSO (UK) plc	Developments in the corporate finance function
Derek Lewis, Finance Director Granada Group plc	
Keith Oates, Finance Director Marks & Spencer plc	
Philip Hughes, Chairman Logica plc	Information technology
Rod Perry, Coopers & Lybrand	
Stuart Turley, Under Secretary Research Board, ICAEW	Future scenarios for the accounting profession
Professor Michael Bromwich, London School of Economics	Accounting standard-setting and corporate reporting
David Damant, Quilter Goodison, London	
Michael Renshall (Chairman, Accounting Standards Committee), Peat Marwick McLintock	
Proffessor Jim Gower, Securities and Investments Board	City regulation
Michael Blane, Senior Counsel Merrill Lynch